Student's Book

Pathway to Science 4

Glue your picture here.

Name

Richmond

rch Skills

Example

wo children need to move a box. They can move it over carpet or over a wooden floor.

he children asked: Which surface will allow the box to ove more easily?

he children answered:
ver the wooden floor because the friction of the wood less than that of the carpet.

he children plan to prove their answer with the ollowing prediction:
The wood has less friction than the carpet.

n order to do the experiment, the children need a small ox, a piece of carpet and a flat piece of wood. Jsing a spring scale, they pull the box first over the vood and then over the carpet.

These are the results:

Material	What happened?
Carpet	It was more difficult to move the box.
Wood	It was easier to move the box.

After reviewing the results, the children related the types of material with the ease with which the box was able to move over them.

They interpreted their data and concluded that wood has less friction than carpet.

What other research questions can you think of?

Richmond
58 St Aldates
Oxford
OX1 1ST
United Kingdom

Pathway to Science Student's Book Level 4

First Edition: 2014
Twentieth Reprint: February 2022
ISBN: 978-607-06-0907-7

Pathway to Science 4 is a collaborative work, created and designed by the Department of Educational Research of Santillana.

Av. Río Mixcoac No. 274, Col. Acacias,
Benito Juárez, C.P. 03240, Ciudad de México

Publisher: Justine Piekarowicz
Editor: Dominic Wright
Art and Design Coordinator: Marisela Pérez
Pre-Press Coordinator: Daniel Santillán

Illustrations: Marcelo Cáceres Ávila, Juan Esteban del Pino Briceño, Antonio Ahumada Mora, Digital Stuff

Photographs: Jorge Quito Soto, César Vargas Ulloa
©REPOSITORIO: Grupo Santillana; ©THINKSTOCK: Digital Vision p. 28 (Anup Shah); Hemera p. 25 (Jeff Gynane); iStock pp. 10 (mdmworks), 16 (Michael Fitzsimmons), 17 (stuckreed), 21 (Dennis Donohue), 22 (gashimo), 24 (mtreasure), 25 (Foto-Kunst-RD), 28 (bpperry), 34 (zanskar), 111 (Andrii Kornev), 143 (Justin Long, Kristoffer Hamilton), 155 (legna69), 158 (DykyoStudio), 160 (estivillml), 161 (john henderson), 167 (emarto)o, (Donvanstaden); moodboard p. 153 (moodboard); Photodisc p. 25 (Digital Vision); PhotoObjects.net p. 167 (Hemera Technologies); Polka Dot p. 52 (Polka Dot Images); Stockbyte. pp. 13 (Comstock), 17 (Stockbyte); Zoonar p. 154 (Zoonar/S.Heap)
🅭🅯 2008 www.birdphotos.com p. 21, Nine-banded armadillo
🅭🅯 2007 Arjan Haverkamp p. 163, *Octodon degus*
🅭🅯 2008 MirandaAdramin p. 163, *Geranoaetus melanoleucus*
🅭🅯🄎 2006 Sandilya Theuerkauf p. 161, Leaf insect
🅭🅯🄎 2007 Piero Sagnibene p. 171, Leaf insect
Cover Design: Erika Martínez
Cover Photograph: iStock (Sherrye Nozaki), Kalapana Ferns

First published by Santillana del Pacífico S.A. de Ediciones

Printed in Brazil by Forma Certa Gráfica Digital
Lote: 808135
Codigo: 292709077 / 2025

One way to answer a question like this is to use our:

Scientific Research Skills

Come with us to discover a fun way to learn science!

Scientific Resea

	Process
Observe and Question	**Observation** You can **obtain information** about an object or a situation by using your five senses.
	Research Questions These come from observing a phenomenon or situation that can be explained by asking questions.
	Hypothesis This is an **anticipated answer** to your research question. It can be proved through experimentation.
	Predictions These are the **results** that you expect to obtain when researching the phenomenon or new situation.
Plan and Conduct an Investigation	**Experimental Procedure** This allows you to check or prove your hypothesis and predictions through exploration and experimentation. In this stage, you gather **supplies** and follow a **procedure** to complete the experiment correctly.
	Results This is the data or information you obtain from experimenting and exploring. You can record and represent the results in various ways. For example, with drawings, diagrams, tables or graphs.
Analyze Evidence and Communicate	**Interpreting and Analyzing the Results** In this stage you should explain the results and **establish relationships** between them in order to explain the research question.
	Conclusions These are the **central ideas** that you will find from analyzing the results. You will compare and contrast them with your hypothesis to verify it. Conclusions often allow you to formulate new research questions.

Introduction

Hi friends!

This book is part of **Pathway to Science**. Follow this pathway to a very special place. This is an educational space for you to develop the skills necessary for your personal and social growth.

- It is full of magic, and everyone is welcome in it. You will find information, texts, pictures and activities presented in a simple and friendly manner. Here you will discover that learning is fun!
- This is a space where we can all learn to share and live together. The activities will help us reflect on our values and learn to respect others.
- It is open to people from all over the world, a place where you can continue to learn more and interactively with the help of the latest technology.
- It is filled with challenges that involve finding solutions, developing math skills and applying calculation strategies that you and your classmates will work on together.

We will be with you every step of the way!
All you need is curiosity and the desire to learn.

Spot and **Kiki**

How is your textbook organized?

Pathway to Science 4 is organized into five units. Here is what you will find in each unit.

Initial Pages

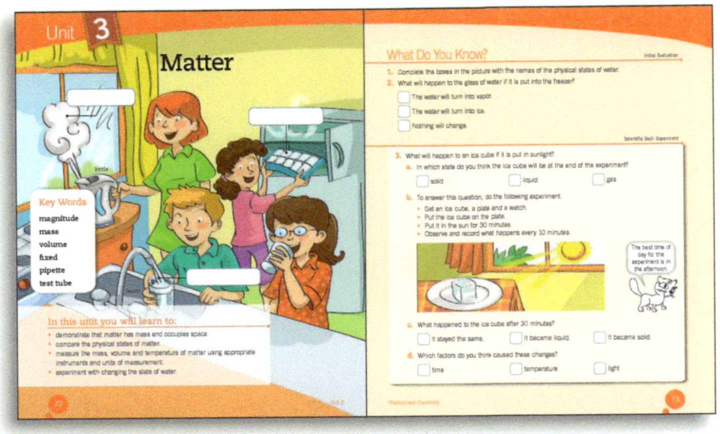

- Number and title of the unit
- Learning objectives
- Initial evaluation

Organized into Sections

- Connecting
  Observe, read and answer
- Exploring
- Practicing
- Summarizing
- Quiz Yourself

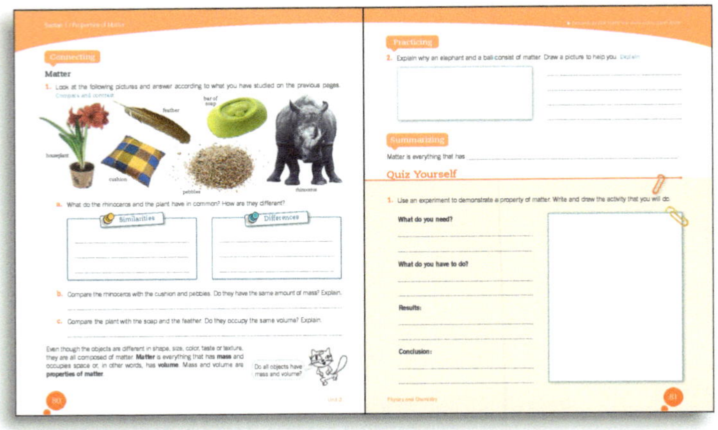

Fun Features

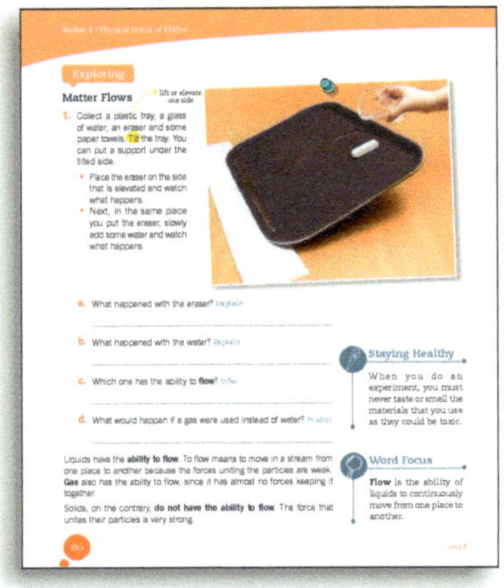

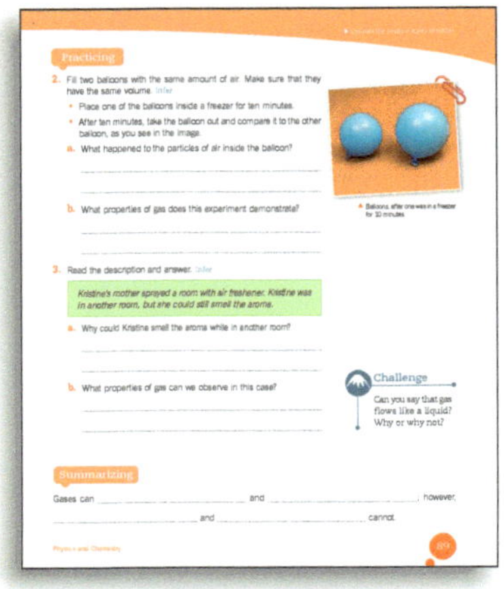

- Education through Values
- Staying Healthy
- Did You Know…?
- Remember!
- Tip
- Word Focus
- Fun Fact!
- Challenge

Evaluation Pages

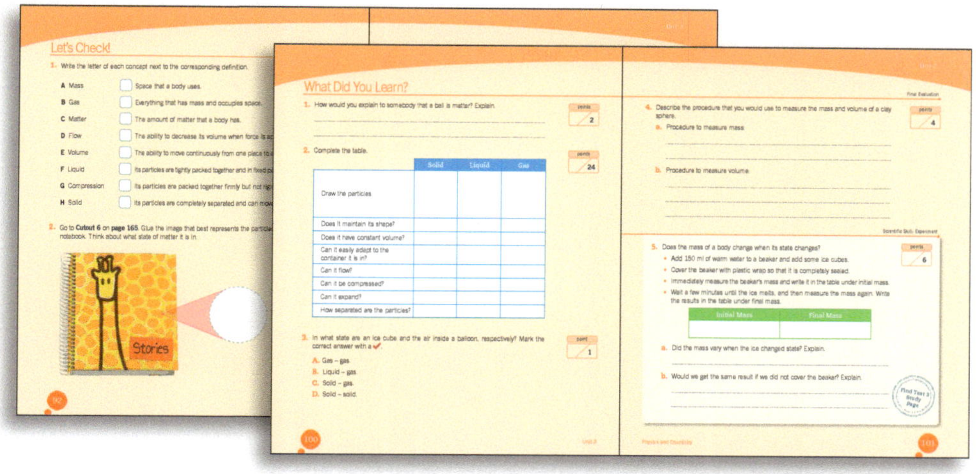

- What Do You Know?
  Initial Evaluation
- Let's Check!
  Intermediate Evaluation
- What Did You Learn?
  Final Evaluation

Special Pages

- Science Lab
- Test Study Pages
  Summary and Review to glue in your notebook

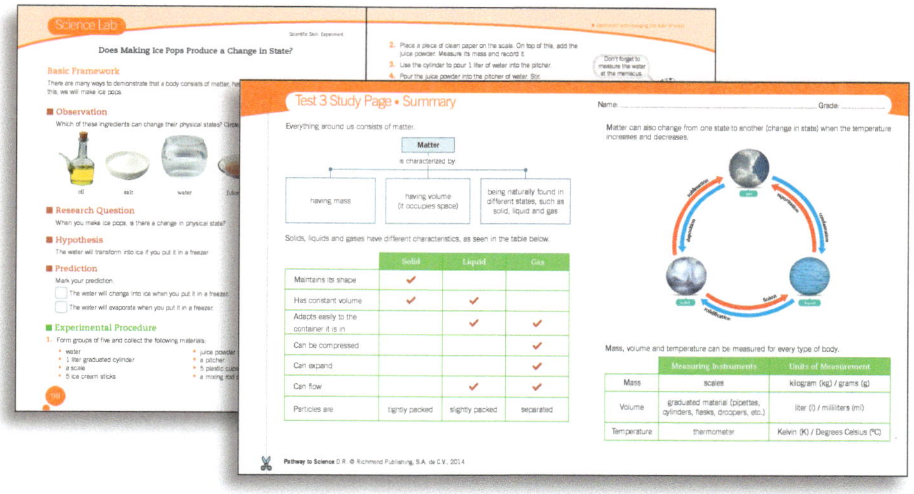

Support Pages

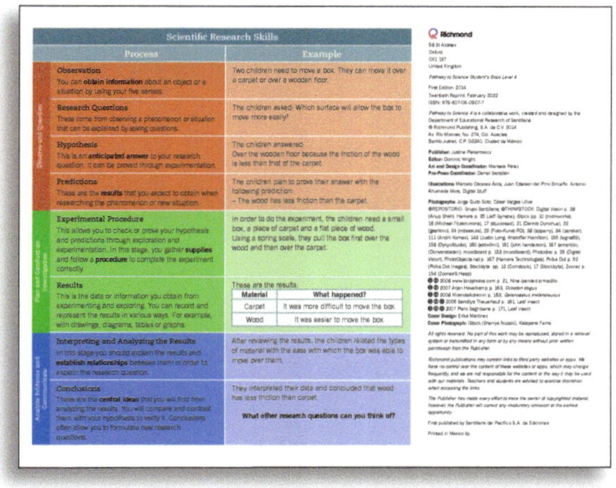

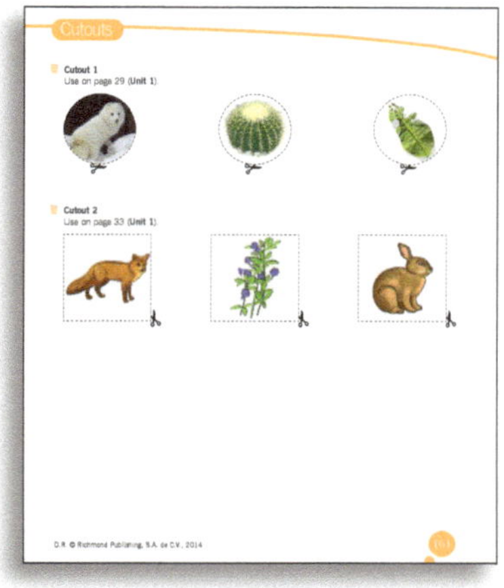

- Scientific Research Skills Foldout
- Cutouts
- Activity Cards

Table of Contents

Unit 1

Living Things and the Environment

Key Words

- classify
- organism
- component
- habitat
- measures
- adapt
- prohibited

In this unit you will learn to:

- recognize that an ecosystem consists of interacting biotic and abiotic components.
- observe and compare the adaptations that plants and animals have made to survive in their ecosystems.
- give examples of food chains in ecosystems, and identify the function of each organism.
- suggest research questions related to the adaptations of birds.

What Do You Know?

Initial Evaluation

1. In the picture, mark the living things with a ✔ and the nonliving things with an ✖.
2. Circle the living things that are not in their natural habitat.
3. What do owls eat? ☐ mice ☐ fruit
4. What do mice eat? ☐ grass ☐ fruit
5. Write the name of the habitat that is represented in each image.

____

____

____

Scientific Skill: Formulate questions

6. The fox in the picture was found by a group of scientists, who then took it to a rehabilitation center because of its hurt paw. Thinking about this situation, which of the following questions would you suggest investigating? Mark with a ✔.

paw: an animal's foot

- ☐ How will the fox be affected by being taken out of its environment?
- ☐ What happened to the fox's paw?
- ☐ What is the relationship between a fox and an owl?
- ☐ What will happen if contaminants are added to the river water?

Section
1 Ecosystems

Connecting

Living Things in Nature

Maybe you have visited some natural environments on vacation, like a forest, a beach or even a desert. These areas are different from each other, but it is very likely that you have encountered common characteristics, too. What are some of their common characteristics? To answer this question, look at the following images.

likely → probable

seaweed → algae

Observing the images, you can see that there are many types of plants in a forest and many types of birds and seaweed at the beach. As a result of the extreme temperatures, low precipitation and poor soil in the desert, there are fewer plants and animals. As you can see, in these three cases there is one characteristic in common: the presence of living things. **It is possible to find living things in the majority of natural environments**. However, you can also find them in artificial environments.

1. Look at the following image and answer.

a. What living things can you see?

b. Is the environment natural or man-made?

c. How many groups or sets of living things do you see?

d. To classify the components of this area, what criteria would you use?

man-made → artificial

The Organization of Living Things

In nature, it is possible to see different levels of organization:

Population: This is a set of living things of the same species that live in the same area at the same time. The penguins in the picture are an example of this.

Community: These are populations that live in the same area at the same time. For example, penguins live together with fish, sea lions and other organisms.

together → in combination

Ecosystem: This refers to a community of living things and their environment, and all the interactions that occur between them.

Word Focus

A **species** is a group of living things with similar characteristics that have **fertile** offspring when they reproduce.

offspring → babies

Practicing

2. Give an example for each level of organization of living things. Exemplify

Population	Community	Ecosystem

Summarizing

In nature, living things interact with each other, and it is possible to organize things as populations, communities and ecosystems.

Connecting

An Ecosystem and Its Components

Look at the following image of an ecosystem.

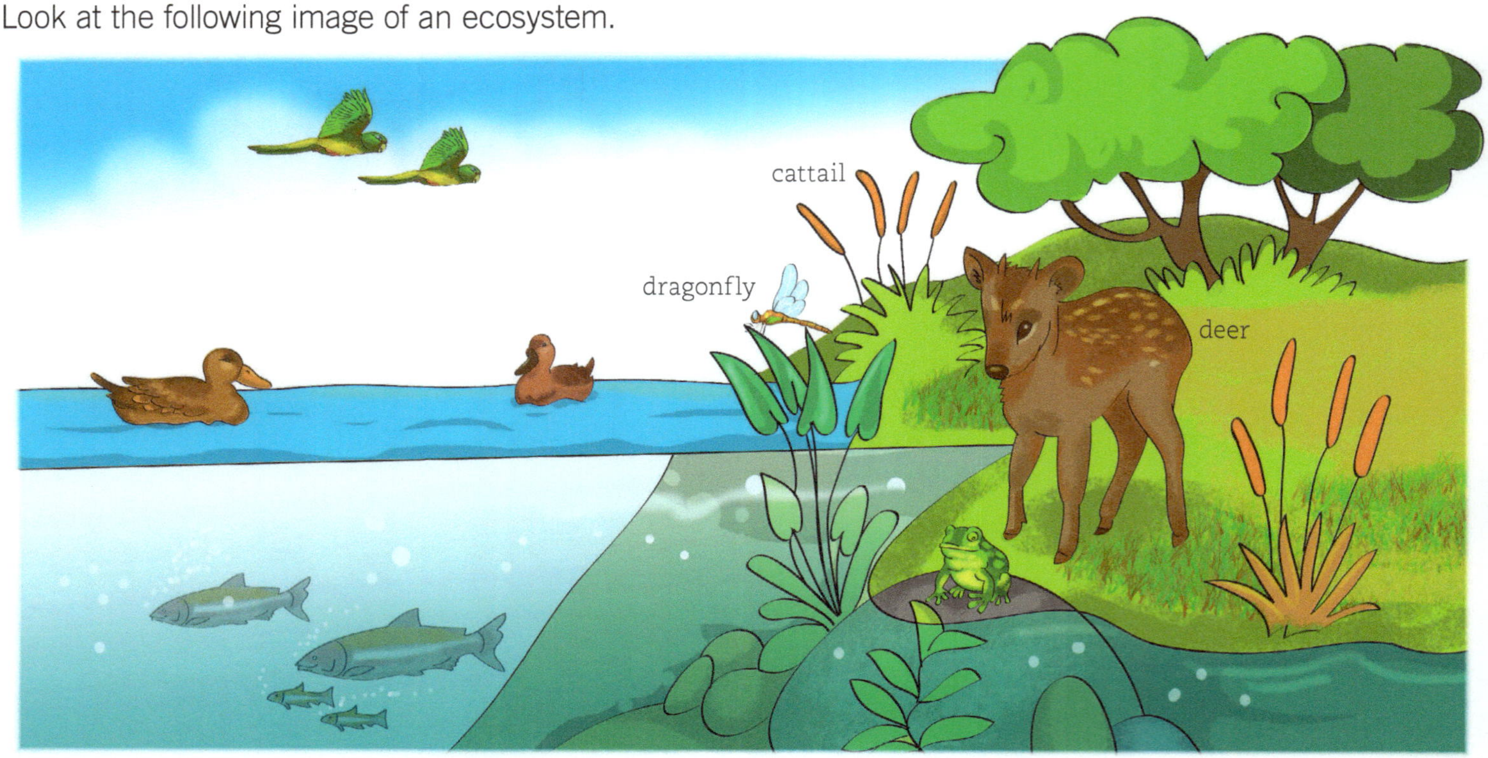

How could we classify the components of an ecosystem? If you look at the image, you will see that there are always two fundamental components: **biotic factors**, which are all living things in an ecosystem, and **abiotic factors**, which are all the nonliving things in an ecosystem.

Biotic Factors

The biotic factors of an ecosystem are **all the living things that live in it**. Different types of plants, animals, fungi and bacteria are all biotic factors.

Tip

Inert and nonliving aren't the same. Nonliving things have never been alive. Inert things don't move.

Abiotic Factors

Abiotic factors are **all the nonliving things in an ecosystem**, like water, air, rocks, light and temperature. All these factors are necessary for living things to live and develop.

In an ecosystem, there is not a single organism that exists isolated from its environment: an organism may not interact with other organisms, but it always interacts with the abiotic factors that surround it.

separate

Biotic and abiotic factors always **interact**.

Practicing

1. Circle the biotic factors in orange and the abiotic factors in blue in the ecosystem below. Recognize

Summarizing

Ecosystems consist of biotic and abiotic factors. Biotic factors are all the living things, and abiotic factors are all the nonliving things.

Connecting

Interactions in an Ecosystem

There exist many forms of relationships between living things in ecosystems. For example, a cow interacts with the grass by eating it. A bird interacts with a tree while making a nest in its branches. Some interactions that can occur between two organisms are:

place to lay eggs

Competition
This is when two organisms **compete** for the same resource, like food or shelter. The lions and cheetahs in the picture are competing for food.

protection from weather or danger

Predation (Predator–Prey)
This is when one living thing eats another for food. A living thing that eats another for its nutrients is a **predator**, and the consumed animal is the **prey**. In the picture, the iguana eats the insect, and the birds eat the worm.

Mutualism
In this case, two living things **mutually** benefit. In the picture, the bee obtains food from the flower, and the bee helps the flower reproduce by transferring the **pollen** that sticks to its body and legs to other flowers.

Living things also interact with the abiotic components of the ecosystem. For example, when animals breathe, they interact with the air around them, and some animals interact with the rocks, twigs and soil to make nests. What do you interact with?

small sticks

Types of Ecosystems

It is possible to encounter many different types of living things and diverse ecosystems if you observe nature. Although many different types of ecosystems exist, there are three main types.

- **Aquatic ecosystems:** Living organisms develop and interact in water, such as oceans, lakes or rivers.
- **Terrestrial ecosystems:** Living organisms develop and interact on land.
- **Mixed ecosystems:** Living organisms develop and interact in areas where water meets land, like on the coast and wetlands.

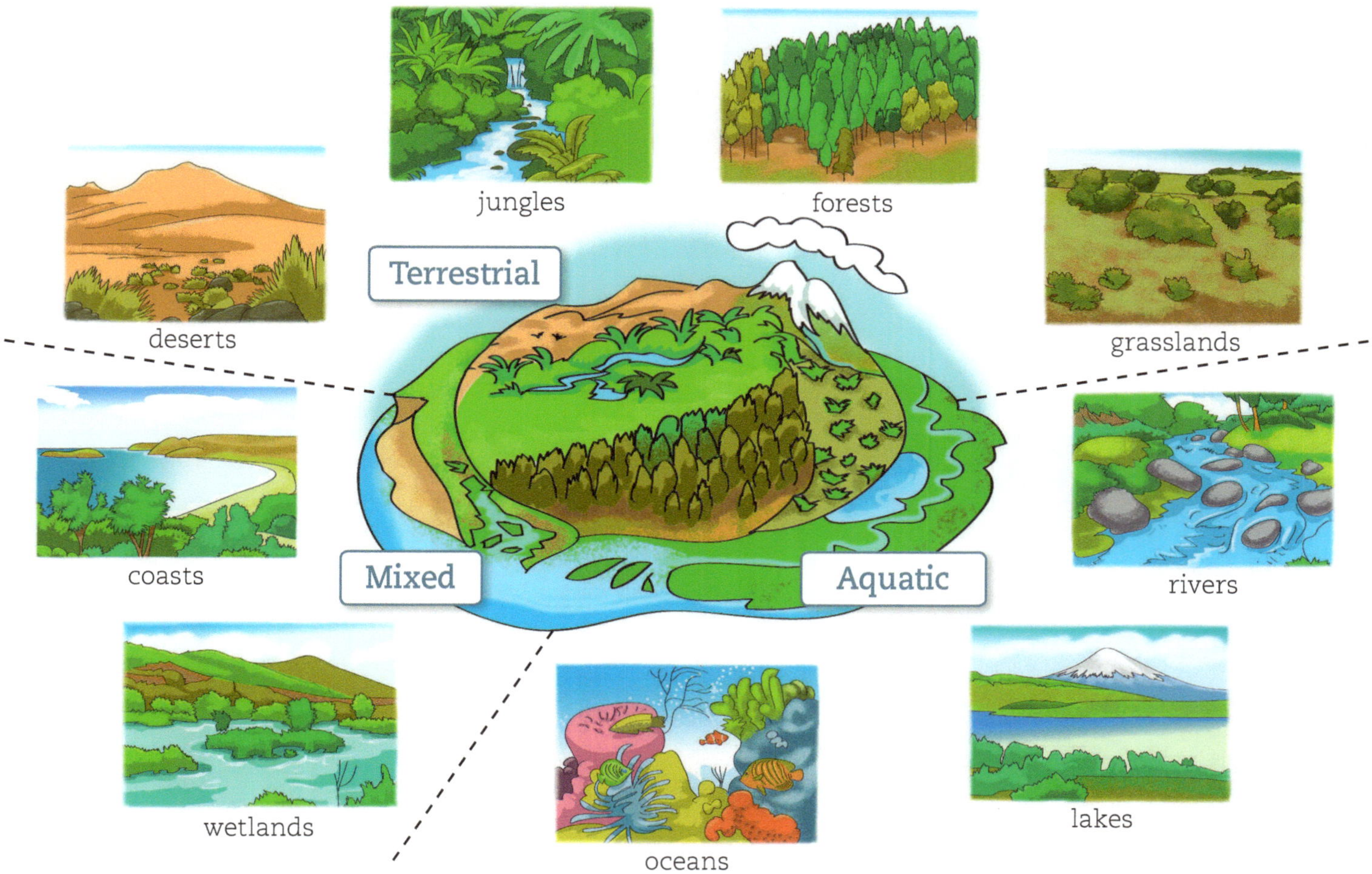

▲ Ecosystems are characterized by their biotic and abiotic factors.

Did You Know...?

Forests, wetlands, deserts and other types of ecosystems are classified as **biomes**. For example, grasslands are a terrestrial biome.

Education through Values

We should all be respectful of nature since any interference, like logging, can alter the natural equilibrium.

logging: harvesting trees

Practicing

1. Write the type of interaction below each picture. Identify

______________________ ______________________ ______________________

2. Look at the following images of ecosystems and mark the correct type. Identify

○ aquatic
○ terrestrial
○ mixed

○ aquatic
○ terrestrial
○ mixed

○ aquatic
○ terrestrial
○ mixed

Summarizing

In ecosystems, the biotic factors always interact—for example, through predation, competition and mutualism. There are also interactions between biotic and abiotic factors, like birds building nests. There are three main types of ecosystems: aquatic, terrestrial and mixed.

Quiz Yourself

1. Look at the ecosystem, and then complete the table with three biotic and three abiotic factors.

Biotic Factors	Abiotic Factors

2. Write the type of interaction shown in each picture.

praying mantis

______

bee

______

bear

______

Section

2 Adaptations of Living Things

Connecting

Living Things and Their Environment

When it rains, do you wear special clothes? Can you imagine a plant or an animal doing something similar? That would be very strange! Unlike humans, plants and animals have to adapt to all the conditions in nature, like cold or hot weather. They do not use clothing to keep warm; they have to depend on their body covering.

unusual

It is for this reason that, in nature, living things have developed **adaptations**. Adaptations are structures or behaviors that permit living things to grow and survive in the conditions of their environment.

ways of acting

Conditions Living Things Adapt To

Look at the following images. Which environment does each organism belong to?

environment 1

penguin

cactus

environment 2

Each organism has certain characteristics according to the environment it lives in. It would be unusual to see a cactus growing on ice or a penguin in the desert!

In order to survive in their environment, plants and animals develop adaptations in relation to:

- their form of movement.
- the type of food they eat.
- the attacks of predators.
- the temperature of the environment.
- the quantity of available water.

Challenge

What is your favorite animal? Does it have any adaptations to its environment? Make a poster and show it to the class.

Practicing

1. Match each organism with its environment. Relate

Summarizing

Living things have adaptations related to the environment they live in. These adaptations are structures and behaviors that allow them to live in an area.

permit

Connecting

How Animals Move

The body structures related to movement are a very clear example of how certain animals adapt to their environments.

Animals from terrestrial ecosystems all have feet adapted to the different conditions that they move in.

Many animals from aquatic ecosystems have elongated bodies and fins that permit them to move easily through water. unusually long

Some animals, like birds, have feet but can also fly because they have developed wings and light bones.

Some animals that live in mixed ecosystems have adaptations that allow them to move in water and on land. An example is the webbed feet of some birds and amphibians.

Word Focus

Webbed refers to the structures that connect toes and fingers in some animals, such as frogs and ducks. They are an adaptive function that enable the animals to swim.

Some terrestrial animals, like snakes, do not have feet and therefore drag themselves or slither to move.

Many insects also have wings and can fly.

Teeth and Diet

An adequate diet is one of the most important necessities for animals. The type of teeth an animal has is directly related to the type of food it eats.

Herbivores have large teeth and flat molars to grind vegetables.

grind: reduce to small pieces by rubbing

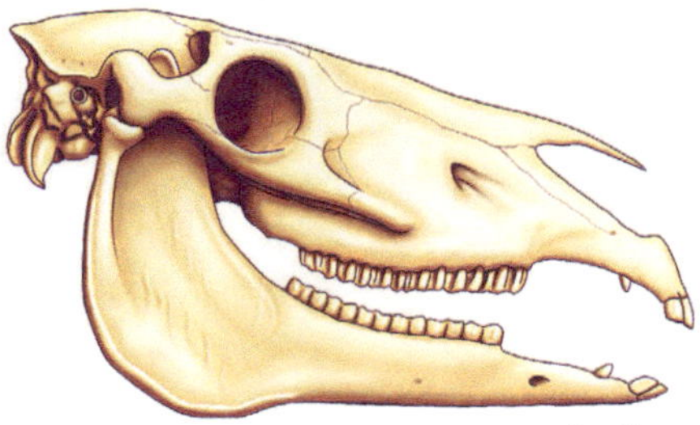

Carnivores have large, sharp fangs that they use to tear the meat of their prey.

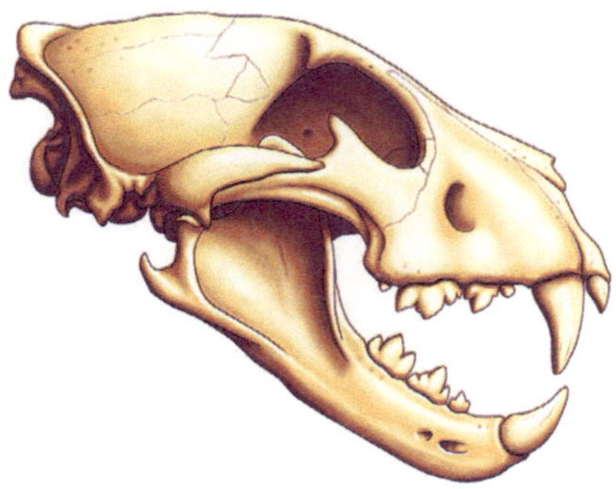

Omnivores have flat teeth and molars in addition to slightly sharp fangs.

slightly: to a small extent

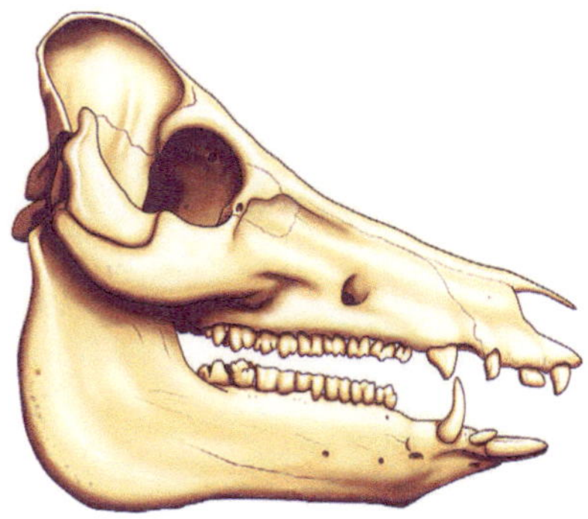

Animal Body Coverings

The body covering of an animal is related to the environment in which it lives and can give it various advantages.

Some animals possess tough body coverings that protect them from the attacks of predators.

tough: strong, durable

Some body coverings protect animals from losing water in very dry environments.

Animals from cold environments have body coverings that allow them to prevent the loss of heat.

How Animals Protect Themselves

absence or deficiency

In nature, animals need to protect themselves from things like cold, heat, lack of water and the attacks of predators. For protection, they develop very specific characteristics and behaviors.

Camouflage

Some animals have colors and shapes that are very similar to the environment in which they live. This allows them to hide from predators or to catch their food. For example, lions use camouflage to help catch their prey.

Mimicry

Many harmless animals have adapted to imitate the colors and shapes of poisonous or dangerous animals. For example, the hoverfly is a harmless insect that has assumed the appearance of bees and wasps in order to avoid possible attacks from other animals.

adopted

Behavior

To **endure** times of cold or scarcity of food, some animals, like the freshwater turtle, hibernate. Others, like the porcupine, raise their spines when they feel threatened.

insufficiency

hard, pointed structures

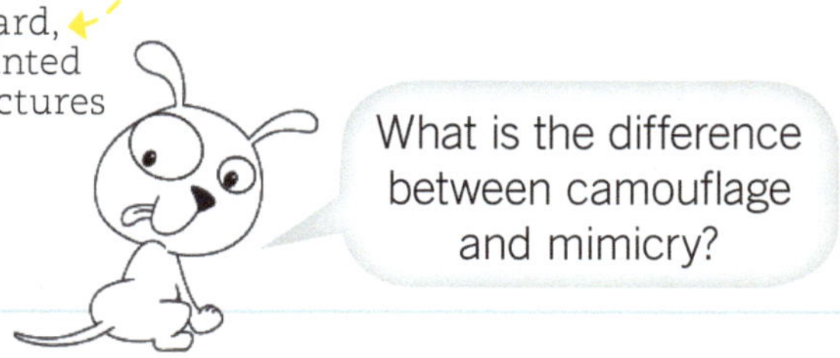

Practicing

1. What adaptations allow animals to move in their environment? Describe

2. Mark with an ✕ the teeth of an animal that eats meat and vegetation. Identify

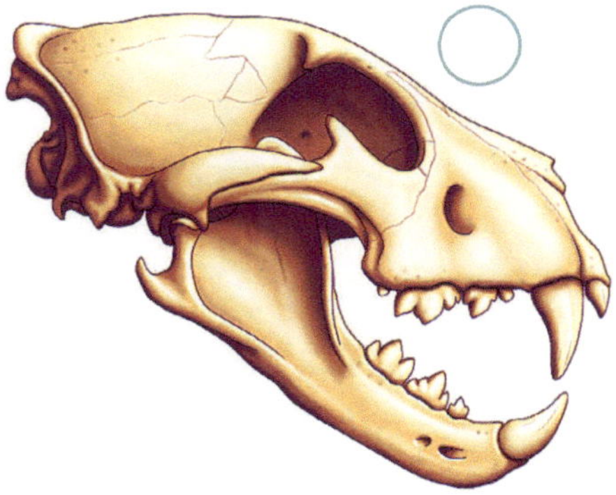

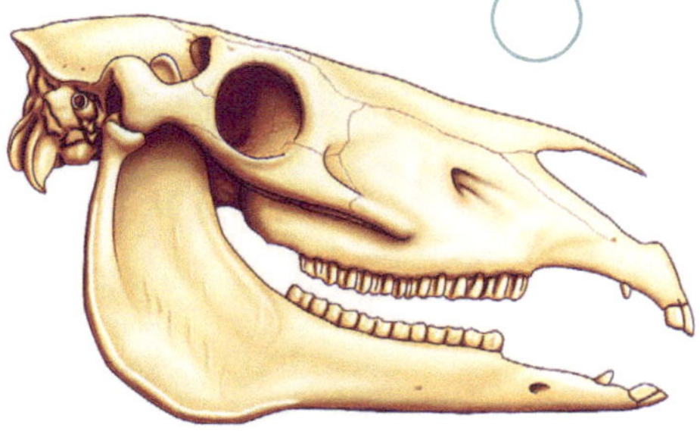

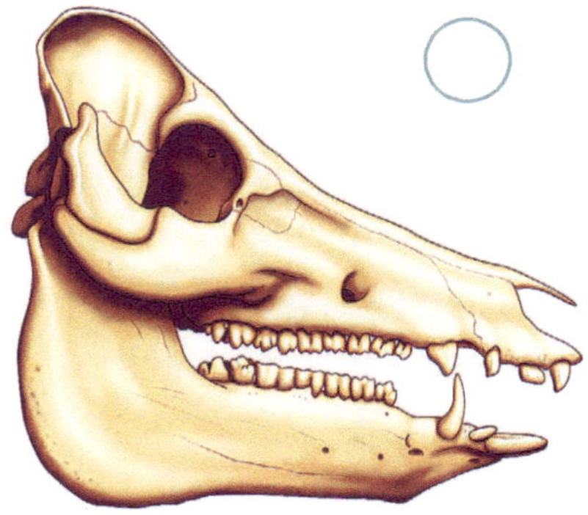

3. Observe the images and explain which adaptations these animals possess in order to protect themselves. Describe

Summarizing

Animals possess different adaptations in order to protect themselves from the attacks of predators, endure the conditions of their environment and feed themselves.

Connecting

Adaptations in Plants

Plants also have adaptations to their environments. Since they do not have teeth to eat nor body parts to help them move, they have parts that **specialize** in capturing the light and water they need.

How do they resist heat?

In dry environments, plants possess thick stems and leaves that have a kind of jelly inside that stores water. These plants are called **succulents**, and the majority have spines instead of leaves in order to reduce water loss and to protect them from animals. The cactus is an example of a succulent.

How do they resist cold?

To resist cold, some plants lose all their leaves to avoid them freezing and being harmed during the cold of winter. These plants are called **deciduous** plants, and they produce new leaves in the spring.

sufficient

How do they receive adequate light?

Some plants grow huge leaves that help them capture as much light as possible.

Have you seen any plants with these adaptations? Where?

Practicing

1. Look at the following plants and write the adaptations that each one possesses in order to survive in its ecosystem. Identify

Summarizing

Plants have different adaptations, like spines or huge leaves, in order to survive in their ecosystem.

Quiz Yourself

1. Write the similarities and differences between the adaptations that the following living things possess in order to survive in their ecosystems.

Why Do the Beaks of Birds Have Different Shapes?

Basic Framework

Birds have different adaptations depending on what they usually eat. One of the primary adaptations is the shape of their beaks.

Observation

Look the pictures.

What shapes are the beaks of these birds?

____

____

Research Question

Mark the research question that is related to the adaptation of birds in order to feed themselves.

- ☐ How is the shape of a bird's beak related to the food it eats?
- ☐ Birds have adapted their beaks in order to feed themselves.

The **research question** should be posed as a question about a situation that you wish to explain.

Hypothesis

The shape of a bird's beak is related to its **diet**.

Prediction

1. If a bird feeds on flower **nectar**, what shape will its beak be? Mark with a ✔.

Experimental Procedure

1. Remove the images from **Activity Card 1** and describe them in detail.
2. What does each bird eat? Remove the images from **Activity Card 2** and match each food with the beak of the bird that eats it.

Results

Complete this table with information from the activity cards.

Beak Shape	Type of Food
1	
2	
3	
4	
5	
6	

Interpreting and Analyzing the Results

1. How did you decide which food matched which beak? Explain.

Conclusions

1. Why do the beaks of different birds have different shapes?
2. What relationship could you establish between the shape of a bird's beak and its food?

Let's Check!

1. Write **A** in each circle if it is an abiotic factor of the ecosystem and **B** if it is a biotic factor.

points
/7

2. Mark the images that show interaction between abiotic and biotic factors with a ✔ and those that show interaction between biotic factors with an ✘.

points
/4

3. Find **Cutout 1** on **page 161**. Glue the living things in the environment that they are best adapted to.

points
/ 5

Environment 1	Environment 2	Environment 3

a. What adaptations does the fox have to help it live in the Arctic? Could it live in Environment 3? Explain.

____

____

4. List the similarities and differences between the adaptations each plant uses to survive in its environment.

points
/ 4

____

____

Food Chains

Connecting

The Role of Organisms in the Environment

In nature, organisms fulfill defined roles that allow ecosystems to function.

The function of each organism is related to the manner in which it obtains the food and energy it needs. There are three types of roles:

Producers	Consumers	Decomposers
They use sunlight and other abiotic factors from the environment to produce their food. All plants are producers and serve as food for other animals.	They obtain energy by eating other living things. Animals are consumer organisms and can be herbivores, carnivores or omnivores.	They transform the remains and waste left by other organisms into substances that can then be used by producers to make food. Fungi and bacteria are examples.

remains: parts left over

Some decomposers are so small that they are invisible to the naked eye, like bacteria.

Fun Fact!

Carnivorous plants are both producers and consumers, as they feed on the insects they trap.

Practicing

1. Complete the table with the names of the organisms in the image according to their role in the ecosystem.
Classify

Type of Organism	Organisms
Producer	
Consumer	
Decomposer	

Summarizing

Living things fulfill different roles in an ecosystem. They are classified as producers, consumers or decomposers.

Connecting

Food Chains

Look at the picture.

How can you relate these living things? The leaves of the bush are food for the deer, the deer is food for the puma, and all of them supply remains and waste that provide nutrients to the mushrooms. These relationships can be shown using a diagram called a **food chain**.

For example, the food chain of the organisms in the picture would be:

> **Remember!**
>
> Just because something doesn't move on its own doesn't mean it is not a living thing.
>
> by itself

In the food chain, the arrows point where the energy flows—in other words, to the consumers and decomposers.

Practicing

1. Find **Cutout 2** on **page 161** and complete the food chain. Draw arrows according to the description. Complete

"In this ecosystem, the fox receives energy from the rabbit, which feeds on the alfalfa."

2. Draw a food chain that includes humans. Apply

Summarizing

A food chain is a representation of one type of relationship between living things in an ecosystem.

What Did You Learn?

1. Use the organisms in **Cutout 3** on **page 163** to make a food chain

points /5

2. Look at the images and write the similarities and differences between the adaptations that each of these living things has.

points /4

3. If two organisms compete for a resource—for example, food or shelter—what is the name of this type of interaction? Mark the correct alternative with a ✔.

point /1

A. Competition.

B. Predation.

C. Mutualism.

D. Mimicry.

4. Look at the following food chain and write the role of each organism.

points
/ 6

plant: ______________________

centipede: ______________________

frog: ______________________

snake: ______________________

falcon: ______________________

a. What type of organism is missing from this chain?

____

____

5. Read the following text and answer.

points
/ 6

The populations of several species of sea turtles have decreased because of the harvesting of their eggs to sell as food. This has put some turtles in danger of extinction.

decreased → reduced in size or quantity

a. Does this situation describe a damaged ecosystem? Explain.

____

b. What measures would you propose in order to protect and recover this ecosystem? Name two.

____

Scientific Skill: Formulate questions

c. Consider the situation above. What research question would you formulate to find the effects of this population decrease on the ecosystem?

____

____

Find Test 1 Study Page

Unit 2

Coordination and Body Movement

Key Words

voluntary

involuntary

expand

contract

exercise

protect

support

In this unit you will learn to:

- identify and describe the structures of the skeletal system and their functions.
- explain body movement and describe the benefits of physical activity for the musculoskeletal system.
- identify the structures of the nervous system and describe their functions.
- discuss the unhealthy effects of alcohol.
- formulate predictions about how muscles work when the arm bends.

What Do You Know?

Initial Evaluation

1. Go to **Cutout 4** on **page 163**. Glue the bones on the girl and the muscles on the boy.
2. Mark the activities that help muscles develop with a ✔.
3. Write the functions of muscles and bones.

Functions of Muscles	
Functions of Bones	

4. Which organs are protected by bones? Name at least three.

Scientific Skill: Formulate predictions

5. Mark the lungs and liver of the person who you think has smoked and consumed alcohol their whole life with a ✔.

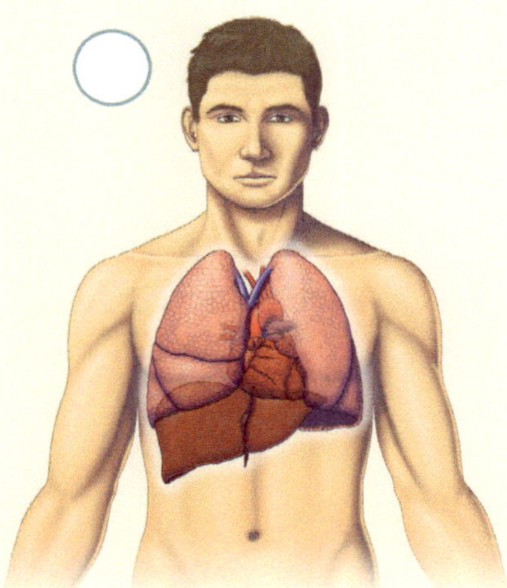

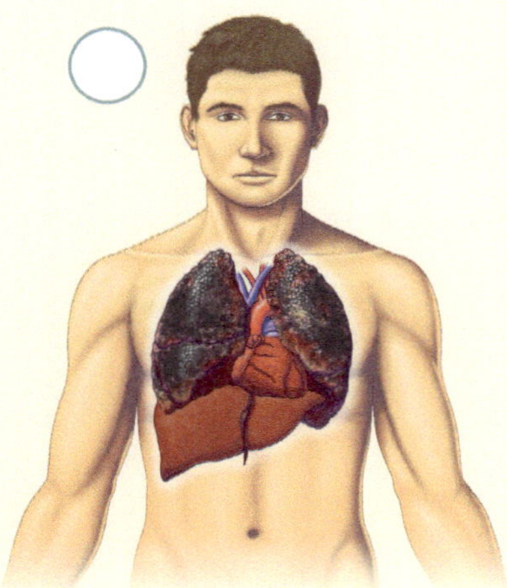

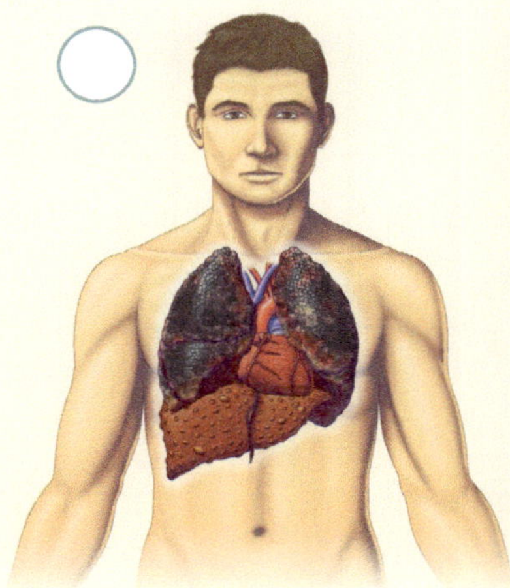

Section
1 The Skeletal System

Connecting

The Skeleton

The boy in the image injured his leg playing soccer. It hurt so much that he decided to go to the doctor. The doctor took an X-ray because he thought the boy might have hurt an **internal** part of his body.

1. What body parts can the doctor see in the X-ray? Identify

____

____

2. What is the function of these parts? Describe

____

____

Bones are the hard parts found inside the body. X-rays allow us to see them, but you can also feel them if you touch your body. For example, you can feel them in your arm.

Bones are part of the **skeletal system**.

Word Focus

An **X-ray** is a picture of the inside of the body, usually of the bones. It is used by doctors to diagnose injuries and diseases.

Understanding the Skeletal System

Have you ever wondered why doctors recommend that children drink a lot of milk? It is because milk strengthens our skeletal system, which consists of **bones** and **joints**.

makes stronger

Bones are rigid structures that give support and strength to the body and protection to the organs.

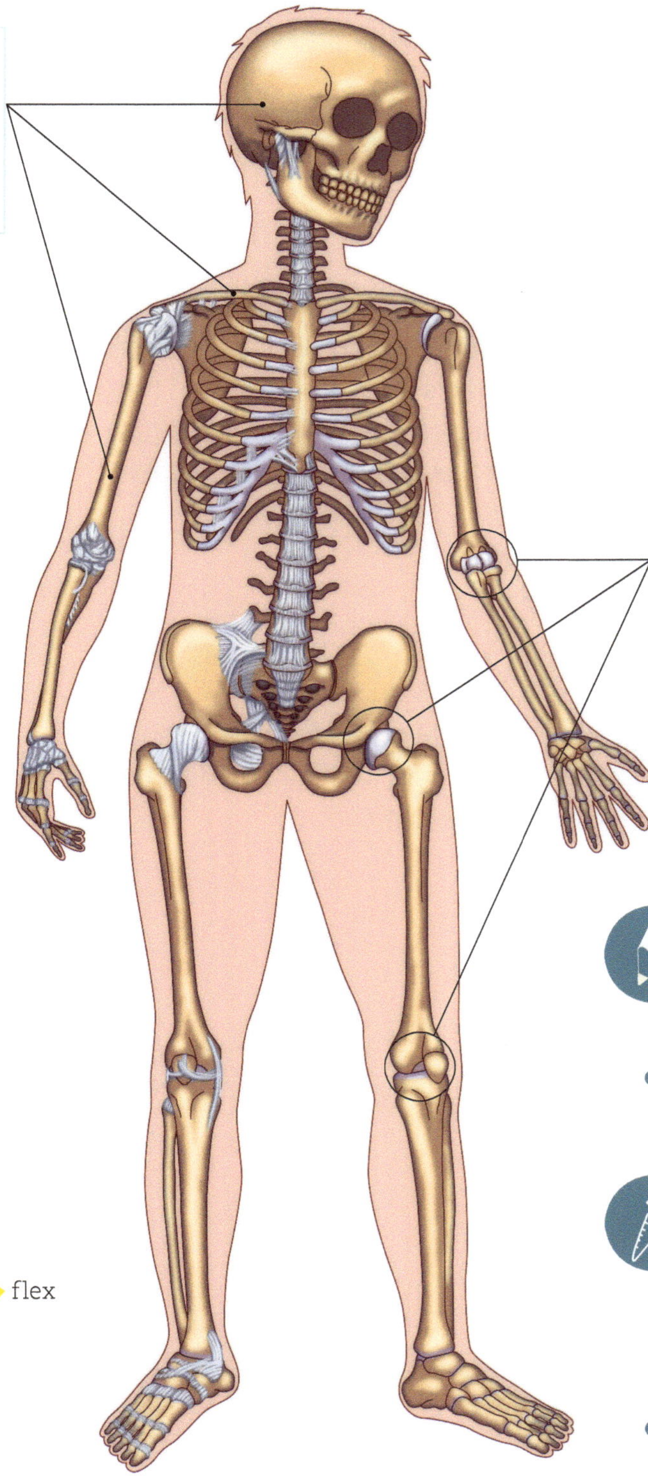

Joints are areas where bones meet, and the majority of joints permit a little movement. Joints include other structures, like **ligaments**, which connect the bones to each other.

Tip

Joints are also called **articulations**.

What do you think would happen if we did not have joints? Could you bend your arm?

flex

Staying Healthy

To take good care of your skeletal system, eat at least four dairy products each day.

The Functions of the Skeletal System

The skeletal system fulfills very important functions in the body.

executes

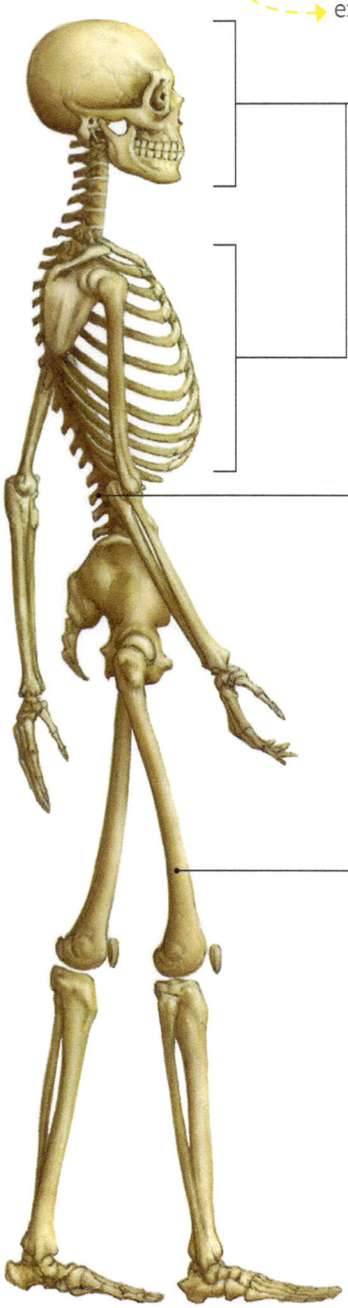

They protect. Some bones protect important organs like the brain, heart and lungs from injury.

damage

They support. Bones are the **pillars** of our bodies. They support the weight of the rest of the body and give it shape.

They allow us to move. Bones work with muscles to allow the body to move.

What would your body be like if you did not have a skeleton?

Word Focus

Muscles are elastic parts of the body that can contract or expand, which allows us to move.

Practicing

3. Complete the diagram with the missing components of the skeletal system. Identify

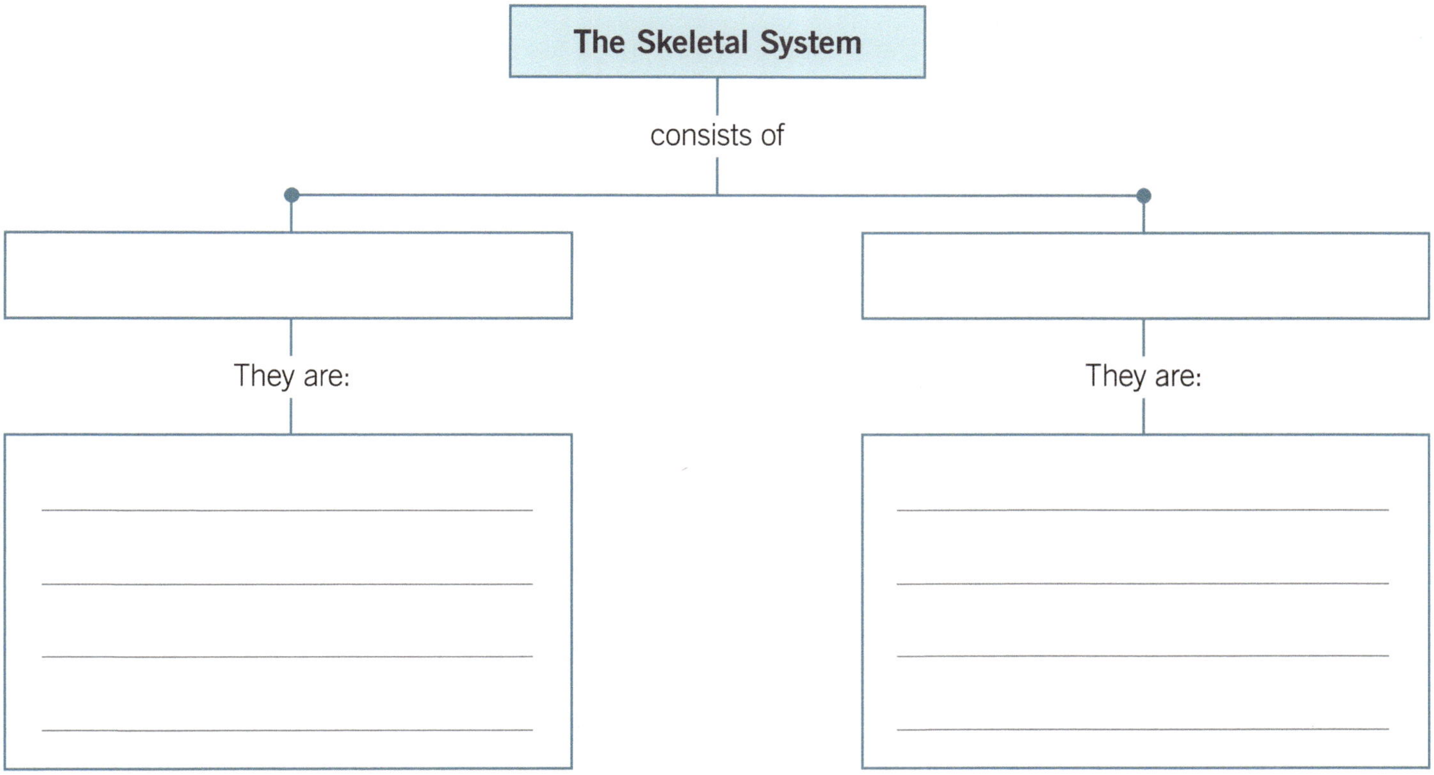

4. What are the functions of the skeletal system? Describe them. Describe

____

____

____

____

Summarizing

The skeletal system consists of ____________________ and ____________________.

It gives support and protection to our bodies. Working together with muscles, it also allows us to

____________________.

Connecting

The Bones in Our Bodies

As we have already seen in this unit, the skeletal system fulfills various functions and consists of **bones** and **joints**. Look at the image and study the names of the principal bones and joints in the human body.

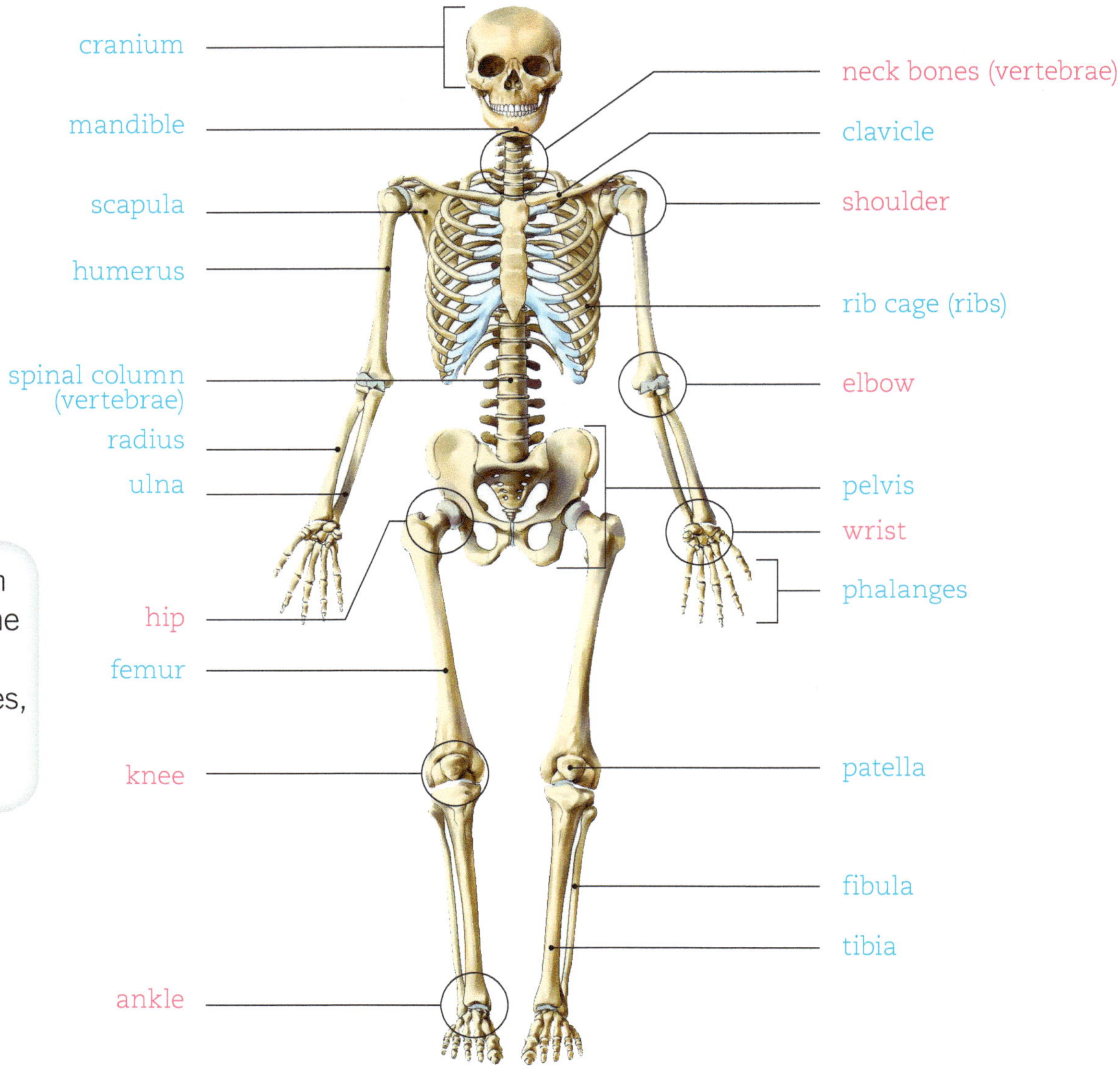

The cranium is not only one bone but a group of bones, just like the pelvis.

Did You Know...?

The longest bone in the body is the femur. An adult's femur can be up to 50 cm long.

Staying Healthy

To keep our bones healthy, we should eat foods that are rich in calcium, **phosphorus** and vitamins.

The Classification of Bones

With your right hand, touch the bones in your left wrist and your left hand. Then feel the bones in your face. Do they all feel the same? In the human body, there are many different types of bones, which can be classified according to their shape. There are four types:

Flat bones: Some examples are the ribs and the bones that make up the cranium.

Long bones: These are found in the arms and legs.

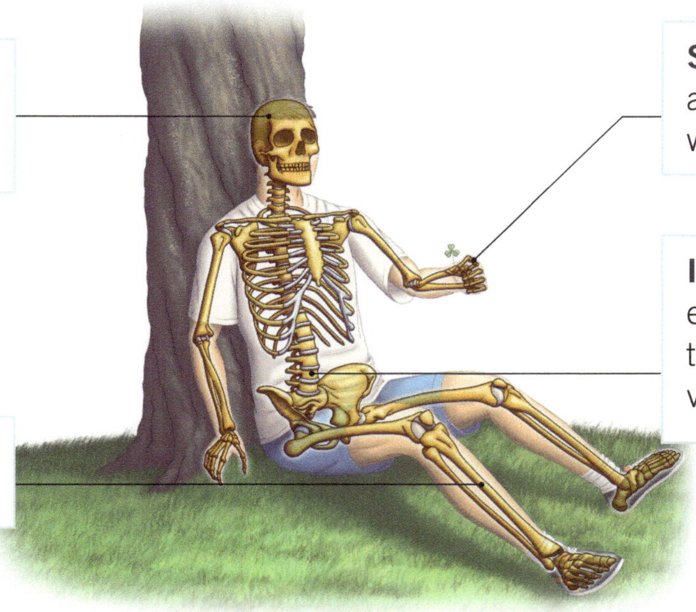

Short bones: These bones are found in the fingers and wrists.

Irregular bones: Some examples of these are the bones in the face and vertebrae.

Practicing

1. Look at the images and classify each bone according to its shape. Associate

Tip

phalanx = one
phalanges = two or more

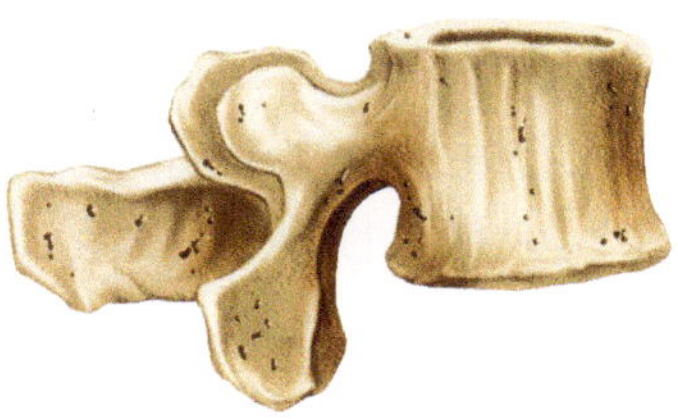

vertebrae

cranium bone

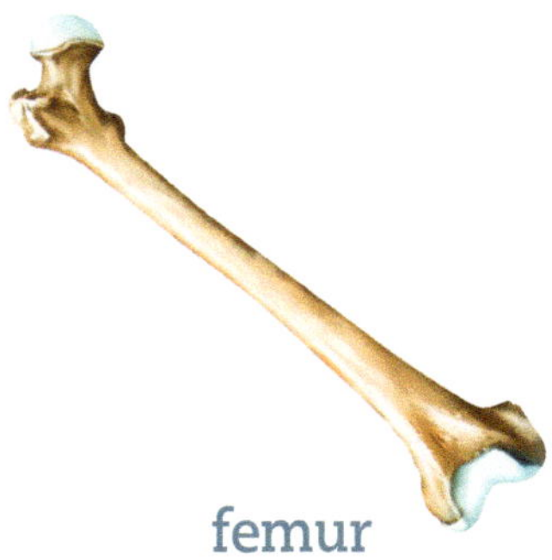

femur

phalanx

__________ __________ __________ __________

Summarizing

The bones of the human body can be classified by their shape as ________________, short, flat and ________________.

Connecting

How Bones Stay Together

Our bodies have many bones that need to stay connected to each other. They stay together thanks to **joints**.

Joints

Joints are connections between two or more bones. They are classified as movable, partially movable or immovable, according to the amount of movement they allow.

Movable joints allow connected bones to move freely. Knees, hips and elbows are all freely movable joints.

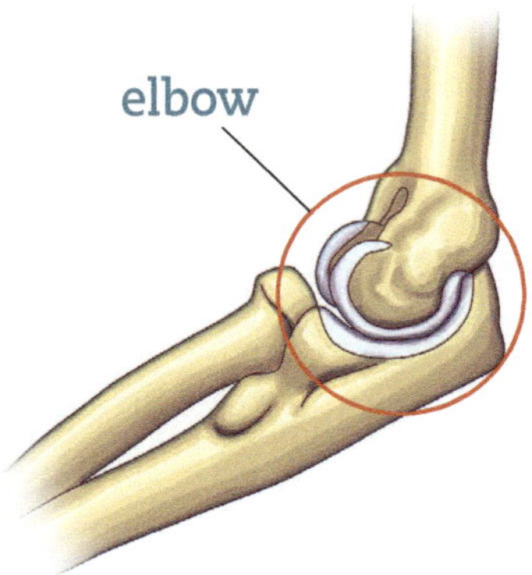

Partially movable joints only allow some movement. The joints between the bones in the pelvis are partially movable.

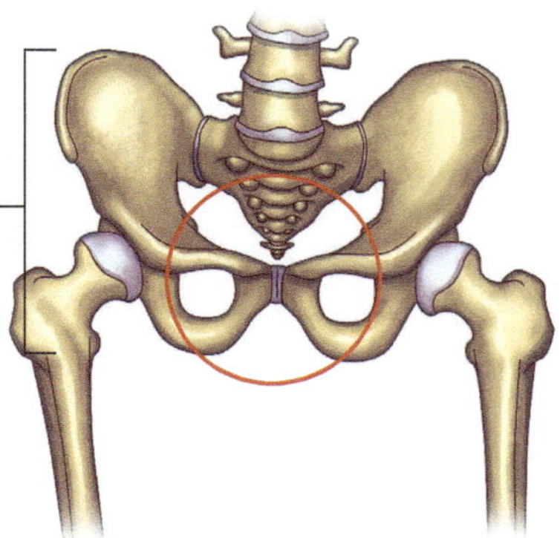

Immovable joints do not allow any movement between the connected bones. The joints that connect the cranium bones are an example of this type of joint.

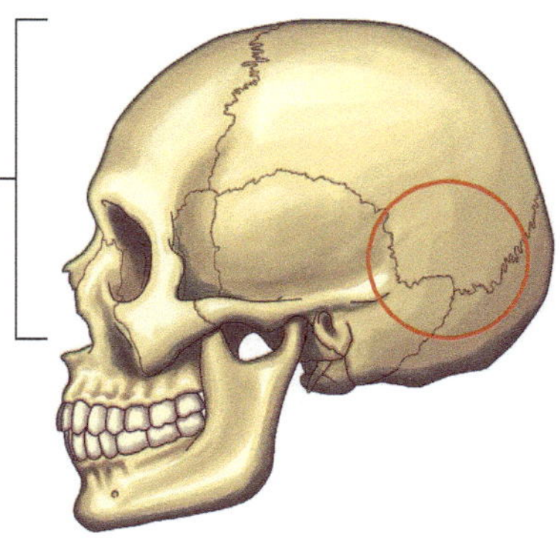

Challenge

Which joints do you use to kick the ball when you play soccer? Act out kicking a ball, and have a partner place a sticker on all the joints of your body that you use. How many stickers did you use?

sticker → adhesive piece of paper

Did You Know...?

Movable joints contain lubricating liquid to make it easier for them to move.

Practicing

1. Write the type of joint in each image. Identify

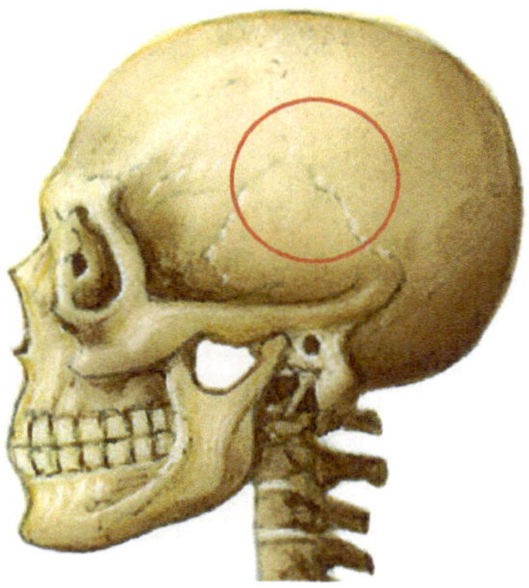

joints in the cranium

____

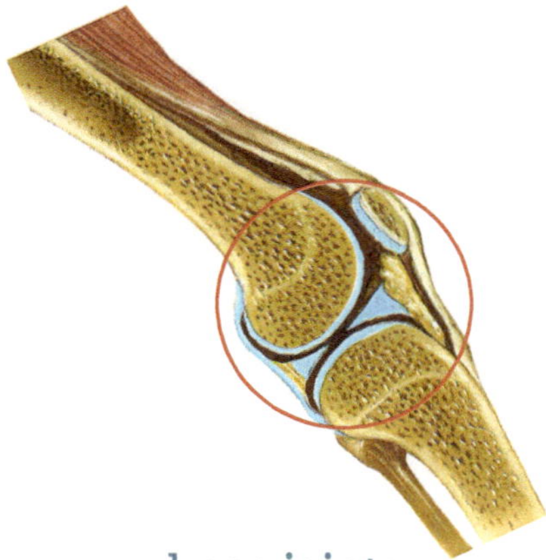

knee joints

____

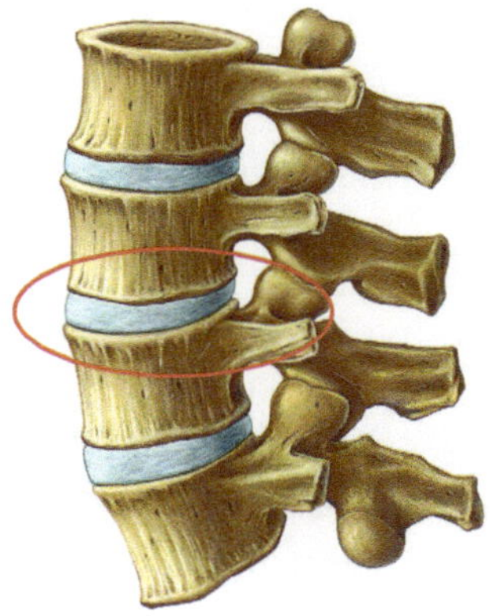

joints between the spinal column

____

2. What is the function of joints? Explain

____

____

Summarizing

Joints are parts of the skeletal system that ______________________ bones.

Quiz Yourself

1. Go to **Activity Card 3** and put together the model of the skeletal system.

a. Color the bones according to their function using this key:

protection support movement

b. What is the function of the skeletal system? Explain.

____

____

Section
2 The Muscular System

Connecting

Muscles and Tendons

In order to move your body, you need the skeletal system, but you also need the **muscular system**.

This system consists of **muscles** and **tendons**.

Fun Fact!

The Achilles tendon connects the calf muscle to the heel bone, and you use it when you walk and run. It is named after a Greek mythological character, Achilles, who was bathed in the river Styx as a baby. This made him invulnerable, except for his heel. He was later shot by an enemy in his one weak spot: the heel!

back part of the foot

Muscles are organs that **contract** and **expand** to create different movements. They are like motors for our bodies. Many are connected to bones, but there are also organs that have muscles as part of their structure, like the heart, stomach and intestines.

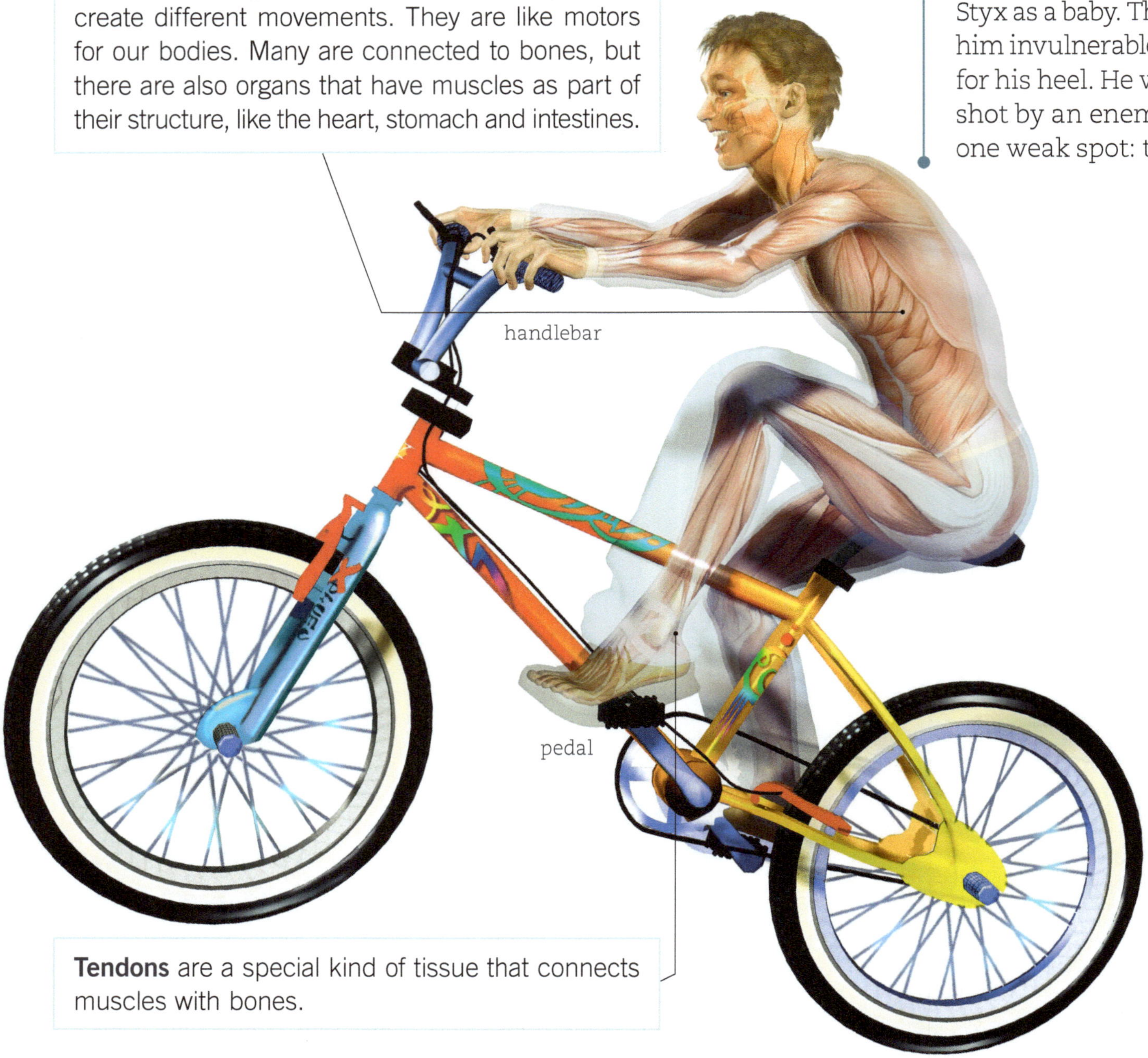

Tendons are a special kind of tissue that connects muscles with bones.

Types of Muscles

Have you ever heard your stomach make a noise after you eat or when you are hungry? This is because the stomach has muscles and moves by itself. These muscles are different from the ones in our arms and legs. What do you think the difference is?

We have two types of muscles in our bodies:

Voluntary

These muscles are controlled by our brain—in other words, they move when we want them to. Examples of this type of muscle can be found in our arms and legs.

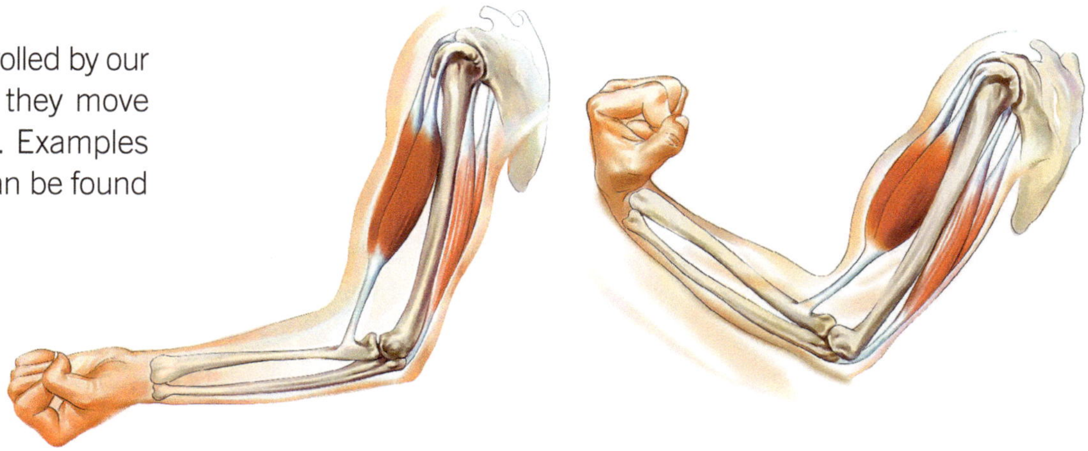

Involuntary

These muscles work without us having to think in order to control them. They are related to functions like blood circulation and the movement of food through the body. They are found in organs like the heart and the stomach.

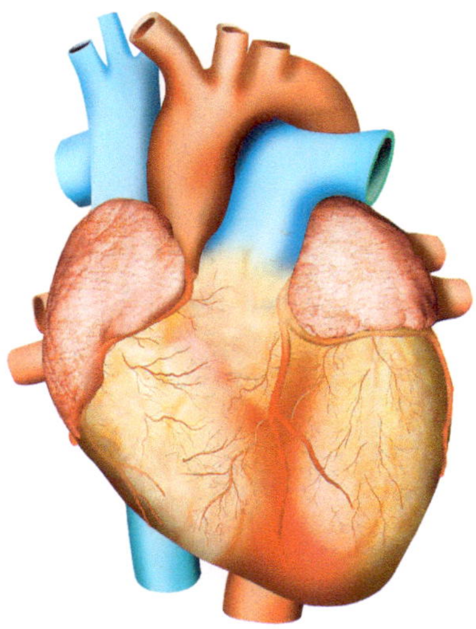

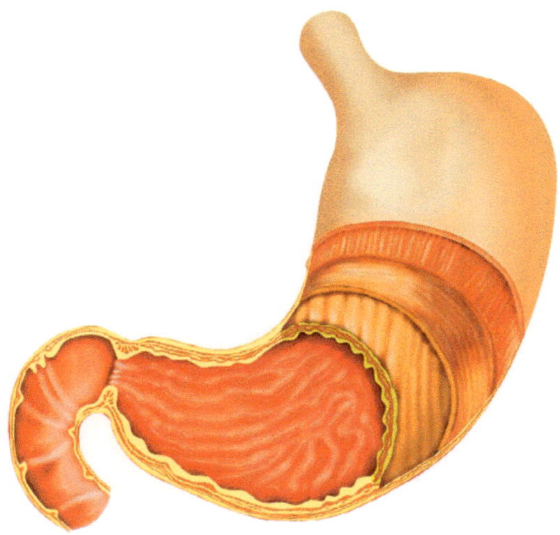

Staying Healthy

Eating foods that are high in fat can block your blood vessels, which transport blood around the body and back to the heart. This blockage can cause a **heart attack**.

What type of muscle do we use when we breathe?

The Principal Muscles in the Human Body

The human body has many muscles, and each one has a specific location and function. The following images show the principal voluntary muscles of the human body.

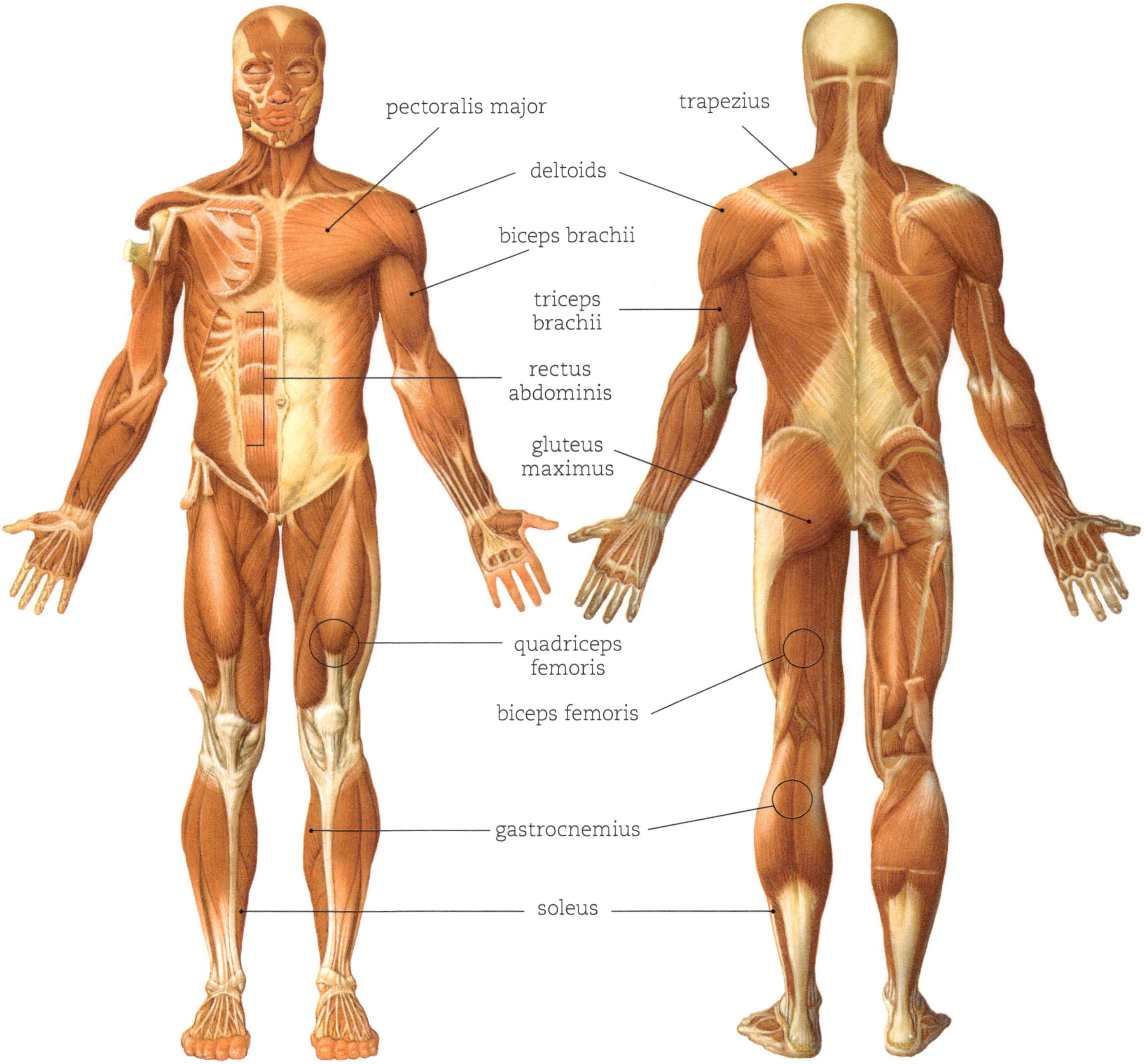

Practicing

1. Write the names of the muscles. Identify

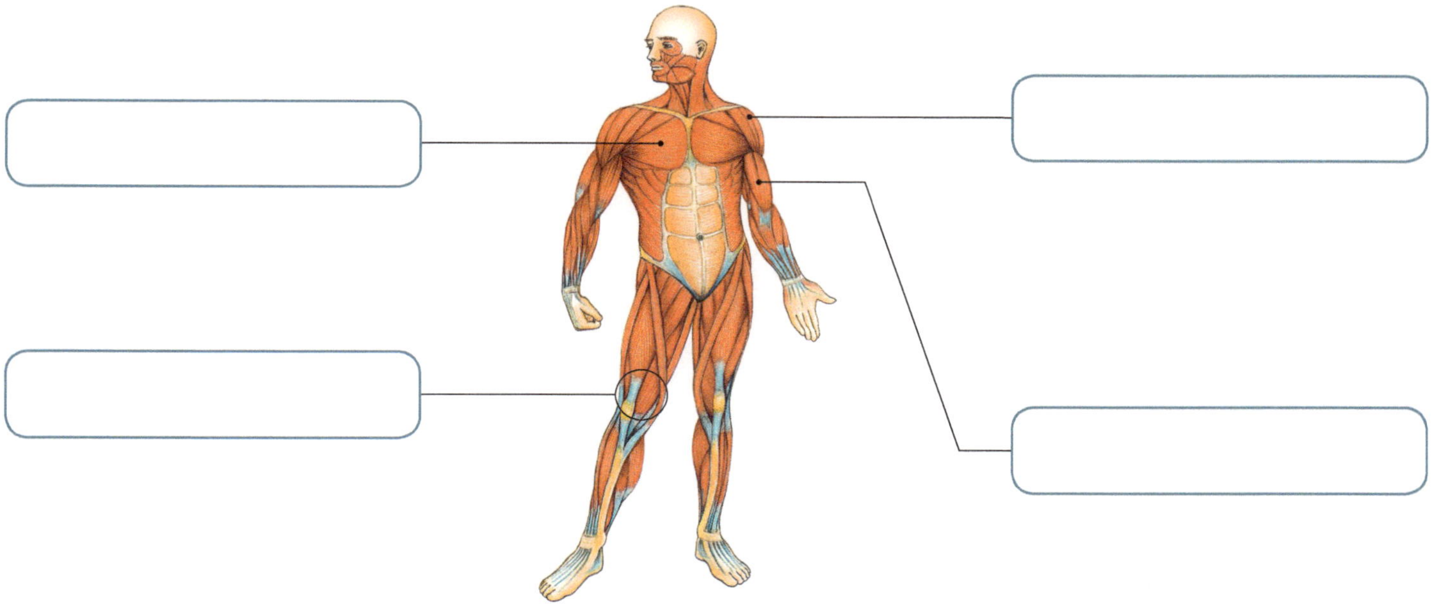

2. Match each movement with the correct muscle type. Relate

Voluntary Muscles	The heart beating.
Involuntary Muscles	Kicking a soccer ball.
	The movements of the stomach.
	Pedaling a bicycle.

3. What is the function of the muscular system? Describe

____

Summarizing

The muscular system consists of ____________________ and ____________________, which together with the skeletal system allow the body to move. There are two types of muscles: ____________________ and ____________________.

Connecting

Body Movement

The actions of the muscular and skeletal systems together allow our bodies to move. Because these two systems are coordinated, they are also called the **musculoskeletal** or **locomotor system**.

Arm Movements

When the biceps brachii contracts, the tendon connecting the muscle to the bone pulls the bone until it meets the muscle. The bone in this case is the radius.

This contraction causes the bone to move, and with it, the arm.

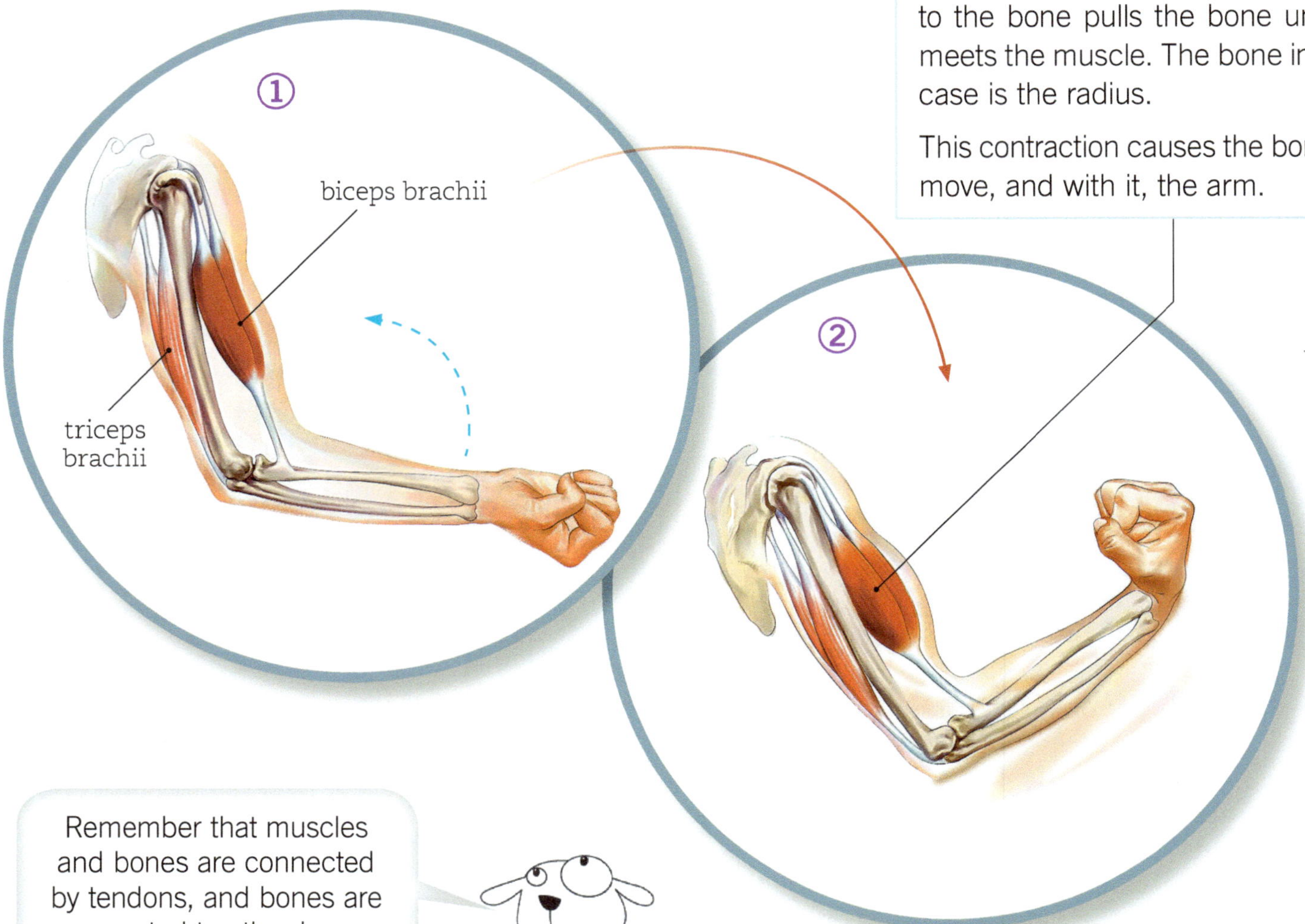

Remember that muscles and bones are connected by tendons, and bones are connected to other bones by ligaments.

In order to move, muscles work in pairs. One contracts and the other expands. Which muscle expands when you move your arm as above?

Remember!

Biceps and triceps are pronounced "bye-seps" and "try-seps."

Leg Movements

Which muscles contract to move your leg? Sit on a chair and raise one of your legs. Which muscles allow you to raise and lower it?

raise → move up

lower → move down

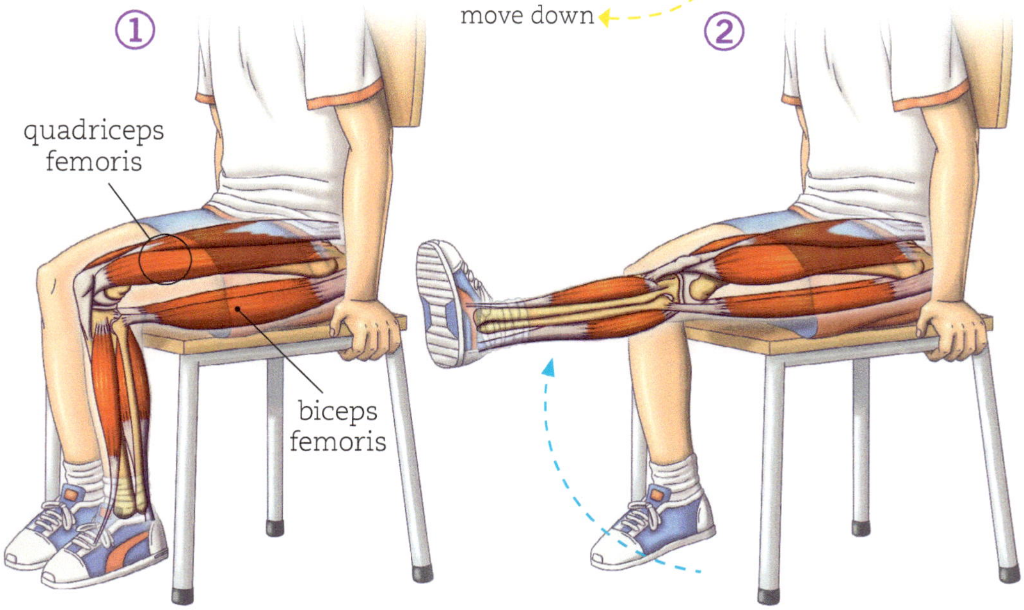

To lift one of your legs, the quadriceps femoris contracts and the biceps femoris expands so that your leg is extended and your foot is off the floor.

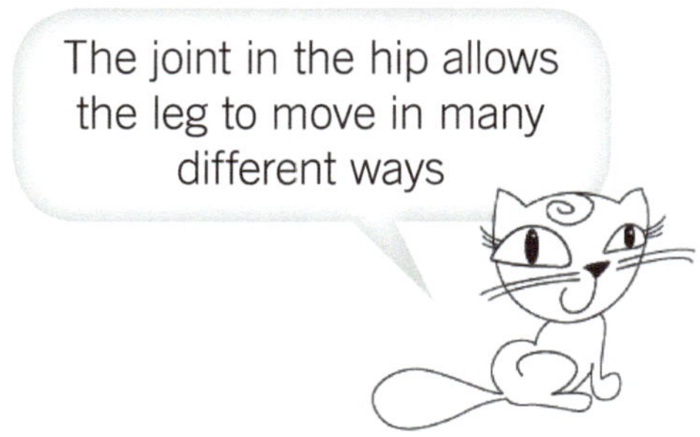

Practicing

1. Which body parts are necessary for movement? Mark them. Identify

muscles	skin	bones	tendons
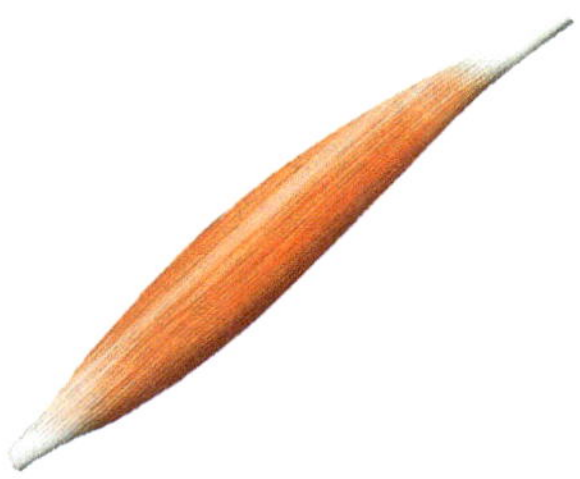	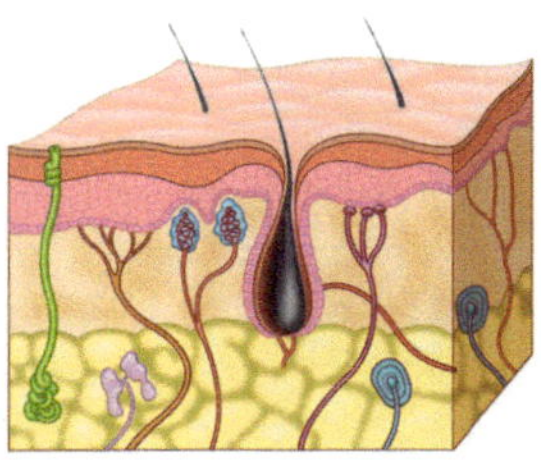	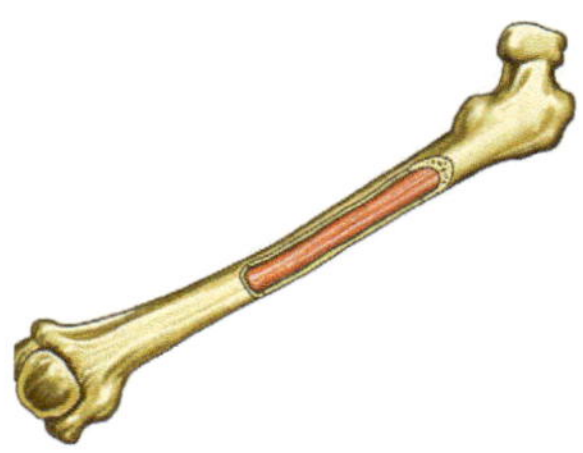	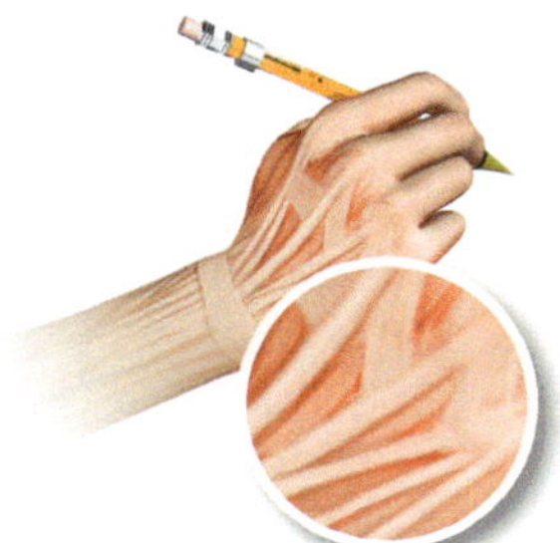
○	○	○	○

Summarizing

In order for our bodies to move, we need the coordinated actions of the ______________________________

____ system.

Connecting

The Importance of Physical Activity

It is very important to take care of our bones and muscles, but how can we do this? Physical activity and exercise help us strengthen and develop our musculoskeletal system by making our bones and muscles more flexible and resistant as well as stronger.

What type of exercise do you like to do?

Riding a bicycle helps you strengthen the bones and muscles in your legs.

Swimming strengthens all your muscles, but especially those in the arms, back and chest.

Running or **jogging** is one of the most complete exercises you can do. It strengthens various muscles, especially in your legs.

Dancing helps strengthen bones and muscles. It also improves your flexibility.

improves → makes better

Exercise and physical activity also help our heart because the heart is a muscle, too!

Staying Healthy

To avoid injuries, you should warm up before doing any physical activity. This helps prepare your bones, muscles and joints for exercise.

Practicing

1. Mark the activities that help take care of your musculoskeletal system. Identify

Summarizing

To take care of and protect our ______________________________, we should exercise by doing physical activities like riding a bike, running, swimming or dancing.

Quiz Yourself

1. Explain the action of the indicated muscle when the girl squats down, as shown in the picture.

____

____

____

____

2. Describe the benefits of physical activity for the musculoskeletal system.

____

____

____

____

____

How Do Your Muscles Work When You Bend Your Arm?

Basic framework

Muscles coordinate in order to move our **limbs**, or extremities. While some muscles contract, others expand. When you flex or bend your arm, the muscles you use the most are the biceps brachii and triceps brachii.

Observation

Look at the following picture.

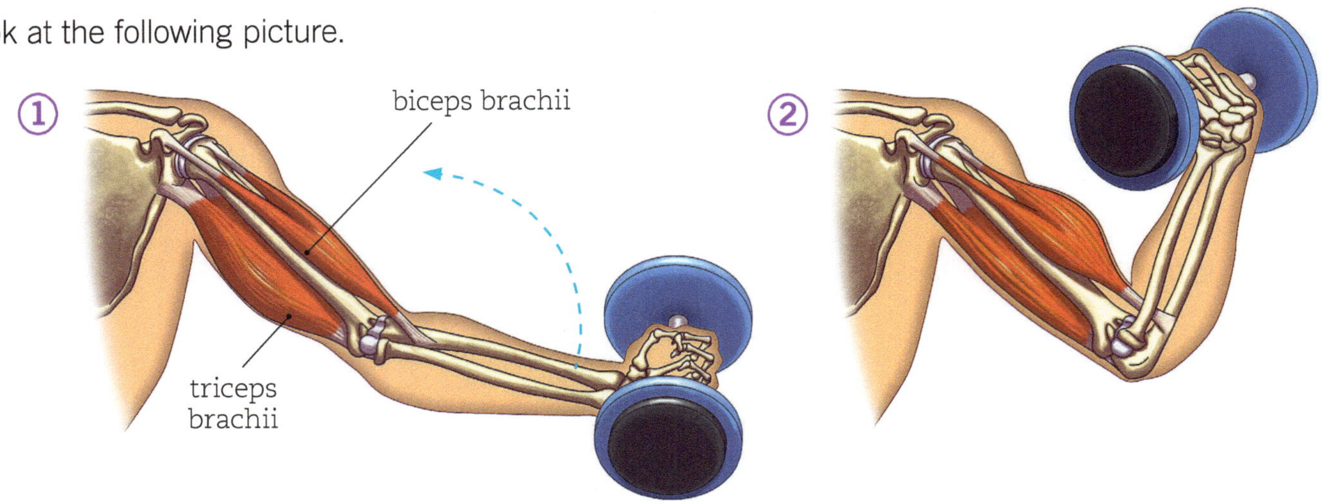

What happens to the arm when it lifts up the object?

____

____

Research Question

How do the biceps brachii and triceps brachii work when bending the arm?

Hypothesis

When the arm bends, some muscles relax and others expand.

Prediction

When the arm bends, what will happen to the biceps brachii and triceps brachii? Think about the hypothesis and mark the correct prediction.

- ☐ If the biceps brachii contracts, the triceps brachii will expand.
- ☐ If the biceps brachii contracts, the triceps brachii will also contract.

Predictions are possible answers about what might happen based on previous knowledge. In this case, they indicate the results you could expect if the hypothesis is correct.

Experimental Procedure

1. Go to **Activity Card 4** and put together the model of the arm.
2. Pull the blue string from point A. Observe how the arm moves.
3. Pull the red string from point B. Observe how the arm moves.

Results

1. How does the arm move in each situation? Describe.

Situation	Movement
Pulling the blue string	
Pulling the red string	

2. Complete the table with the part of the arm that corresponds to each component of the model.

Component of the Model	Part of the Arm
paper	bones
metal fastener	
red string	biceps
blue string	

Interpreting and Analyzing Results

1. When the biceps brachii contracts, what happens to the triceps brachii?

____

2. When the triceps brachii contracts, what happens to the biceps brachii?

____

Conclusions

1. How do the biceps brachii and triceps brachii work when bending the arm? Explain.

____

Let's Check!

1. Write the names of the indicated bones.

points
/ 7

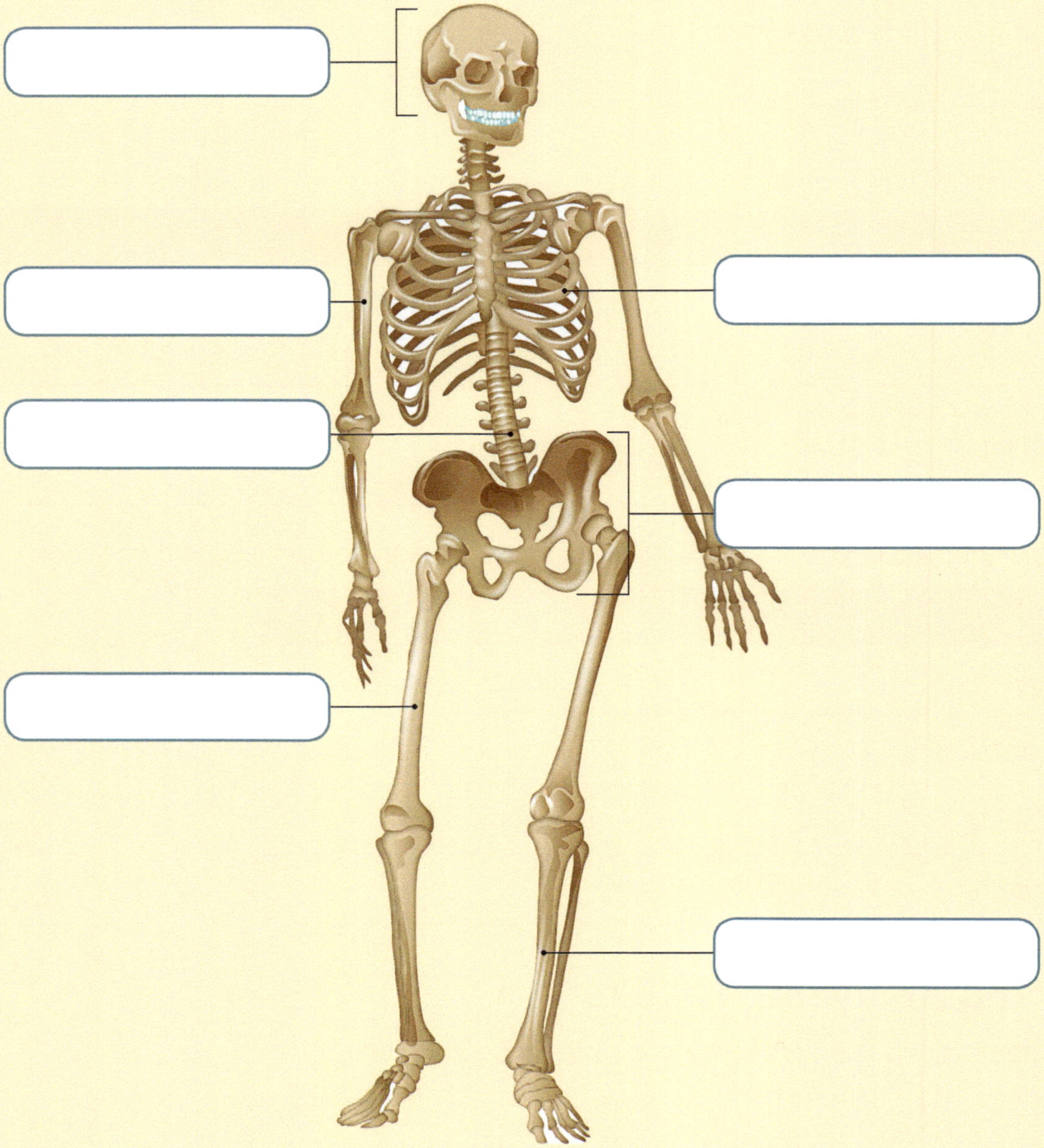

2. What are the functions of the skeletal system? Explain.

points
/ 6

____

____

____

3. Look at the images.

points
/ 4

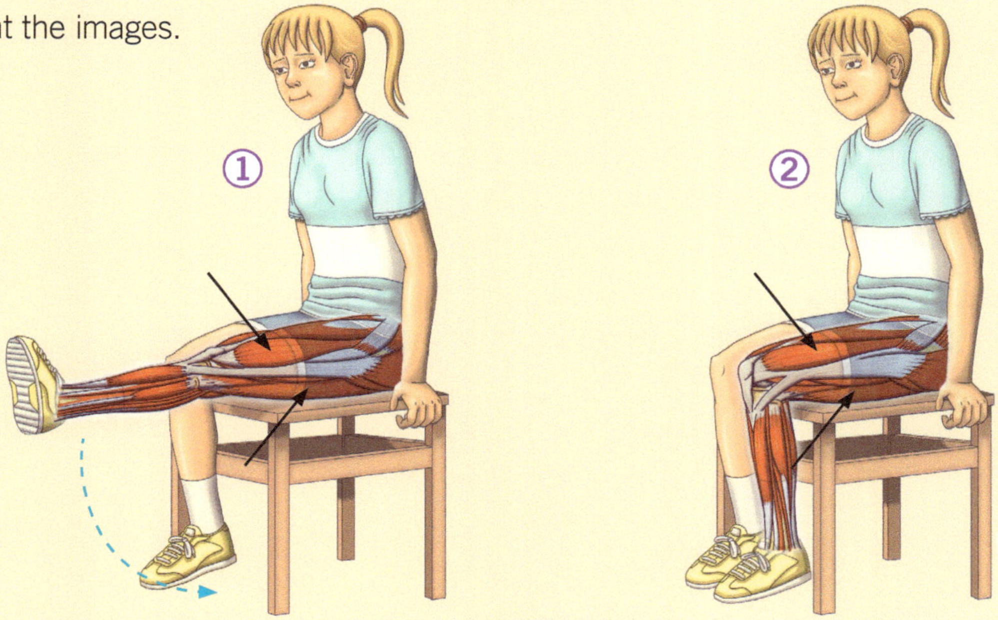

a. What happens to the indicated muscles when raising and lowering the leg? Explain.

____

____

4. Explain the benefits of these activities for the musculoskeletal system.

points
/ 4

______________________ ______________________

______________________ ______________________

______________________ ______________________

The Nervous System

Connecting

Understanding the Nervous System

While you are reading this, one of the systems in your body is working without you knowing it. It is helping you understand what you are reading, moving your eyes, keeping you sitting up straight and even coordinating the muscles in your arm and hand to be able to turn the page. Do you know what system this is? It is very important, and it is called the **nervous system**.

The nervous system is responsible for taking in information from the world around us and interpreting it. It is also in charge of producing and controlling many things in our bodies, such as movements.

The nervous system is composed of:

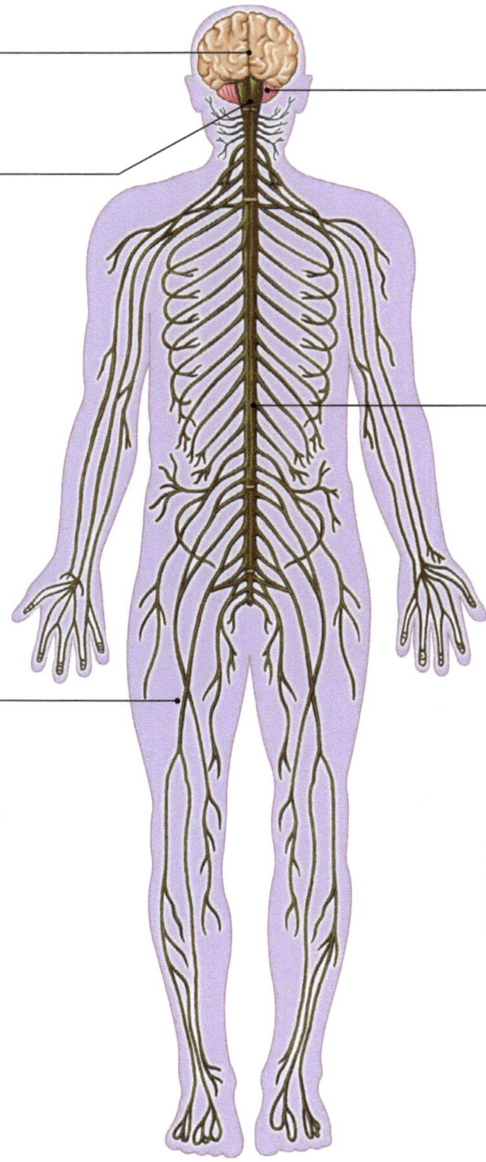

Did You Know...?

The nervous system is divided into two parts: The **central nervous system**, which is the brain and spinal cord, and the **peripheral nervous system**, which consists of the nerves spread throughout the body.

The organs of the nervous system coordinate the rest of the structures in the body.

The Functions of the Nervous System

In order to coordinate the rest of the body, the nervous system receives information, processes it and responds. Consider the following situation:

quickly and unexpectedly

Ray was going to cross the street, but at that moment the light turned red, so he stopped suddenly.

This simple situation shows how the nervous system works.

- **First, it receives information from the sense organs**: Ray sees the red light.
- **Then it processes the information**: Ray understands that it is not safe to cross the street.
- **Finally, a response is formed**: Ray stops and waits for the green light.

Practicing

1. Mark the structures that are part of the nervous system. Identify

- ☐ brain
- ☐ cerebellum
- ☐ tendons
- ☐ brain stem
- ☐ spinal cord
- ☐ joints
- ☐ nerves
- ☐ cranium

2. Describe how the nervous system works when you ride a bicycle. Apply

____

____

Summarizing

The nervous system is in charge of ________________________________

____.

Connecting

The Organs of the Nervous System

Our nervous system consists of various organs that work together. Their work allows us to receive information, process it and respond to it. Observe the following functions of the organs of the nervous system.

Spinal Cord

This organ is shaped like a rope, and it runs from the head to the lower back. It is located inside the spinal column, which protects it. The spinal cord is one way that information travels to and from the nervous system organs located in the cranium. It is also responsible for simple responses like reflexes.

Nerves

Nerves are long fibers that are connected to all parts of the body. They receive information and transmit it to the brain, the spinal cord and the brain stem. They also send orders from these organs to the rest of the body.

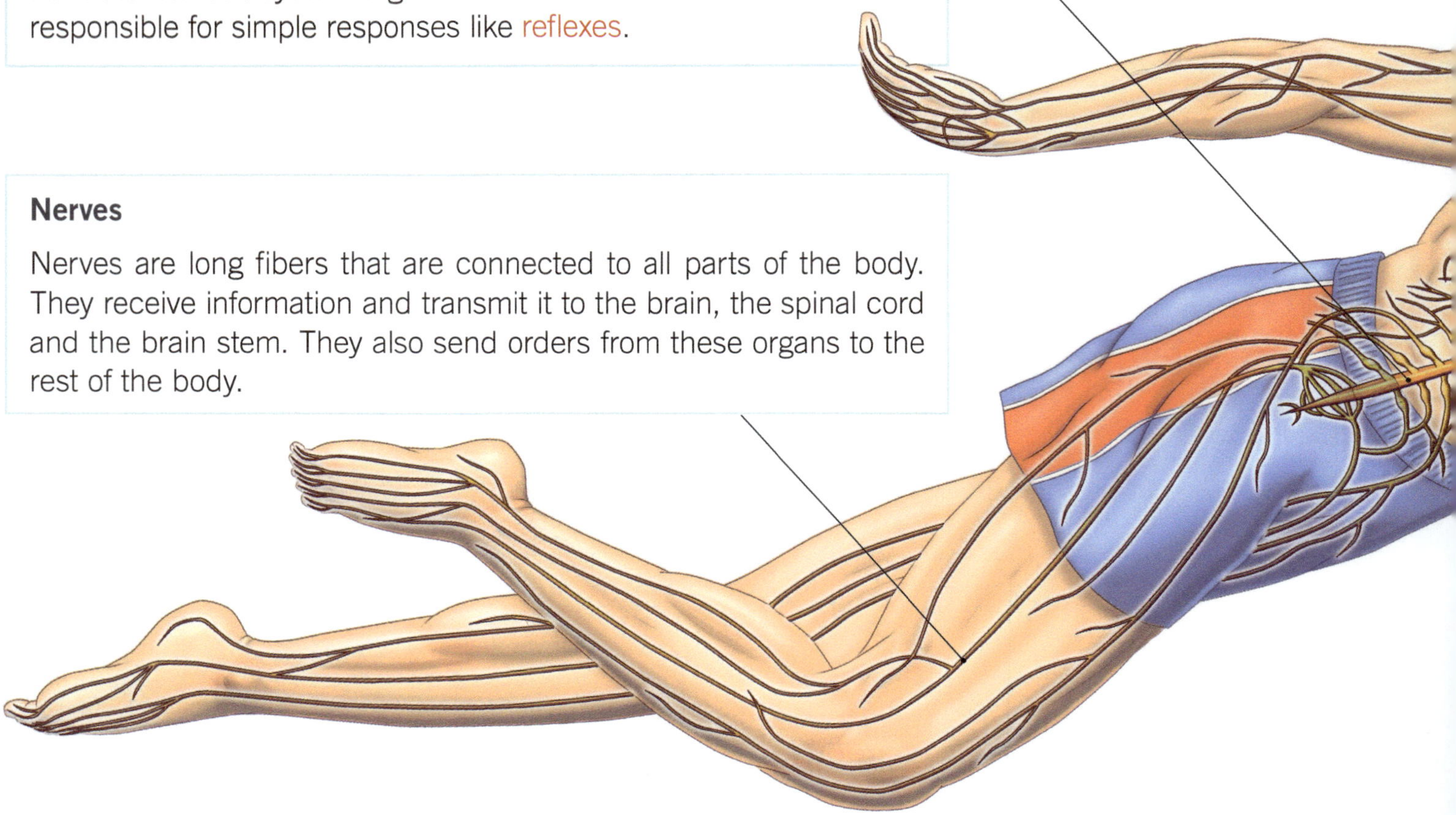

Word Focus

Reflexes are rapid involuntary responses of the body. For example, when you touch something hot and your hand moves away without even thinking about it, that is a reflex.

Fun Fact!

Have you ever hit your "funny bone?" In fact, it is not a bone that makes your arm feel strange, it is the ulnar nerve! It is very close to the skin where it passes over the elbow, so if you accidentally hit your elbow, it is easy to hit your ulnar nerve, too.

Cerebellum

This organ is smaller than the brain and is also protected by the bones in the cranium. It is in charge of coordinating muscles to move and controlling body **posture** and **balance**.

control

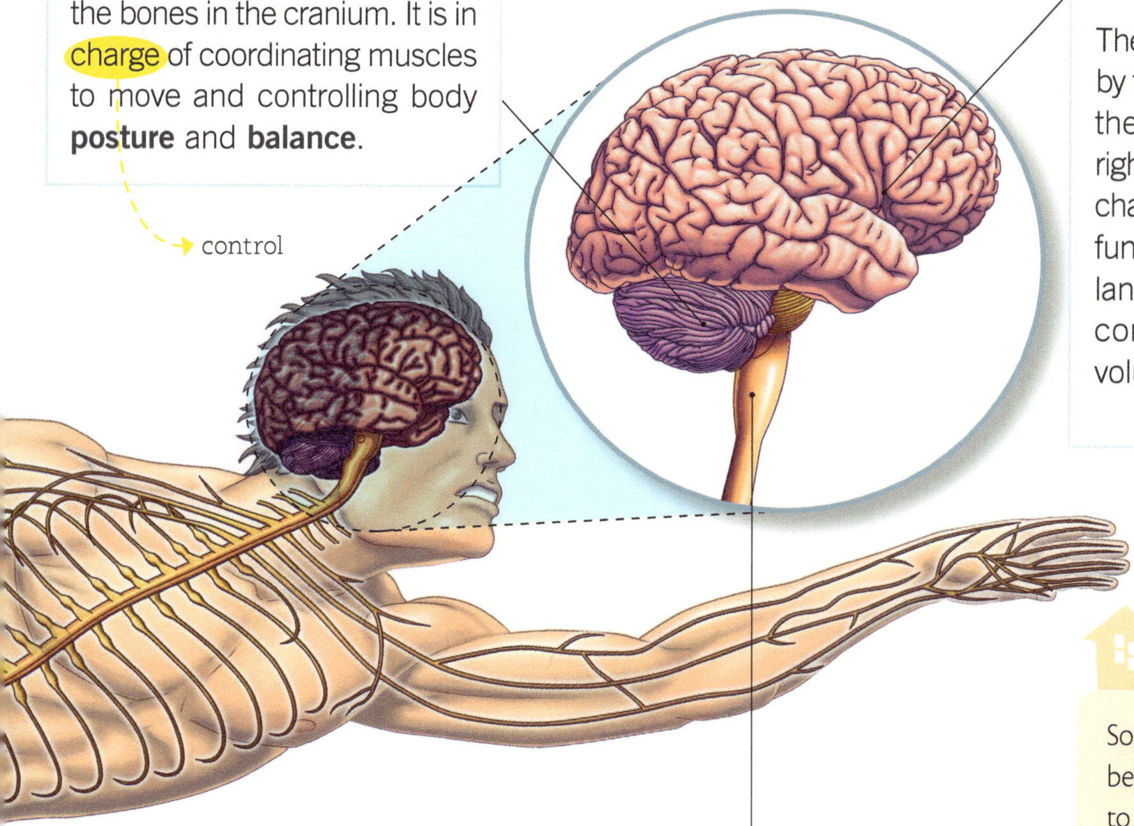

Brain

The brain is the organ protected by the cranium. It has two parts: the left **hemisphere** and the right hemisphere. The brain is in charge of the most complicated functions like thought, memory, language and emotion. It also controls the movements of voluntary muscles.

Education through Values

Some people have disabilities because they have suffered damage to their nervous system. Respect all people no matter what disabilities they might have.

without considering

Brain Stem

This organ is located in the head. It is responsible for controlling involuntary movements like blood circulation, breathing, some eye movements, sneezing, coughing and hiccuping.

Challenge

With a partner, use a stopwatch to test how fast your response time is. Place a coin or a piece of paper on the desk. When your partner says "go," touch the object as quickly as you can. Switch roles with your partner. Who is faster?

Fun Fact!

Each cerebral hemisphere receives information from and controls the movements of the opposite side of the body. Also, they each help you do different things.

Practicing

1. Write the name of each organ and then match it with its function. Relate

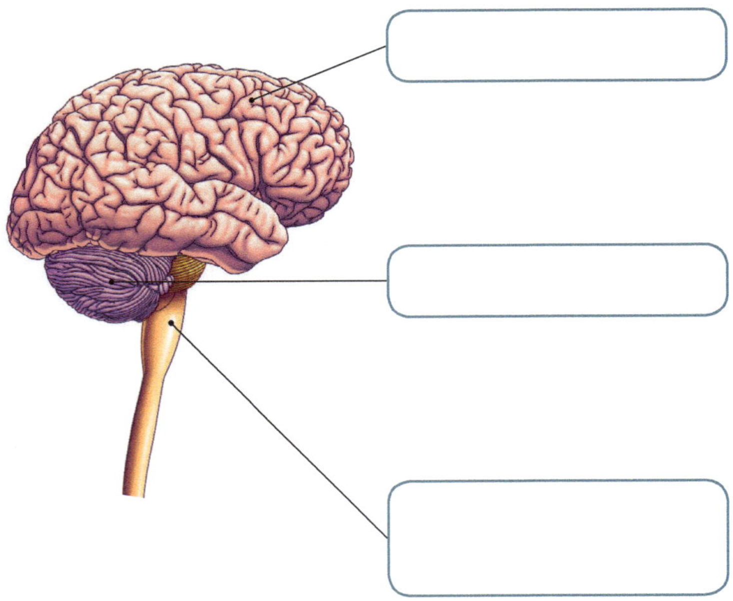

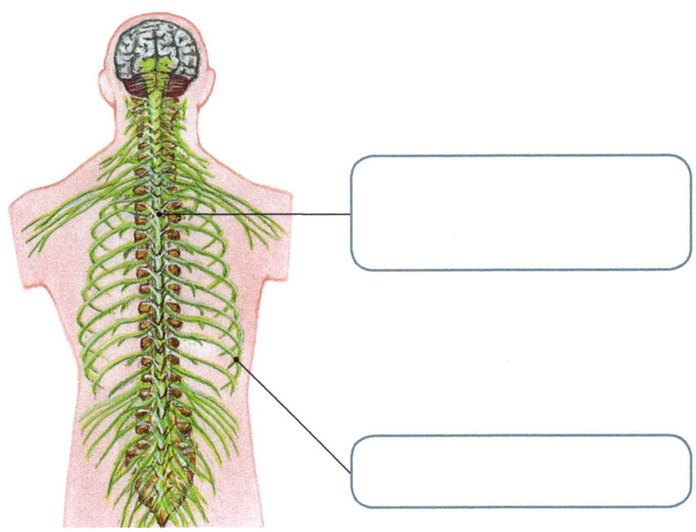

- Controls respiration and circulation.
- Controls things like thought and memory.
- Are all over the body, receiving and sending information.
- Coordinates muscle movements.
- Carries information to and from the nervous system organs located in the cranium.

Summarizing

The nervous system consists of ____

____.

Quiz Yourself

1. Write the name of each part of the nervous system.

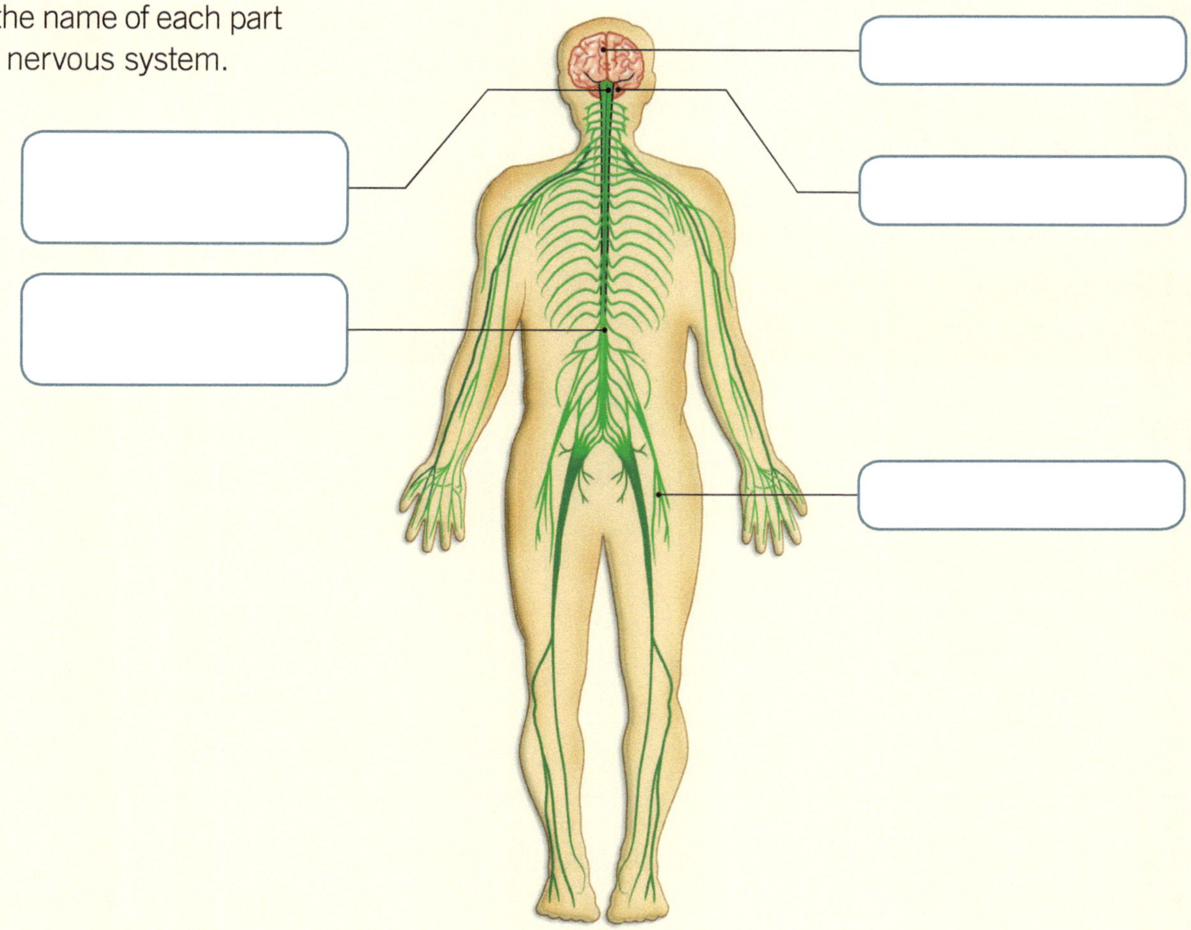

2. Write the function of the nervous system in each situation.

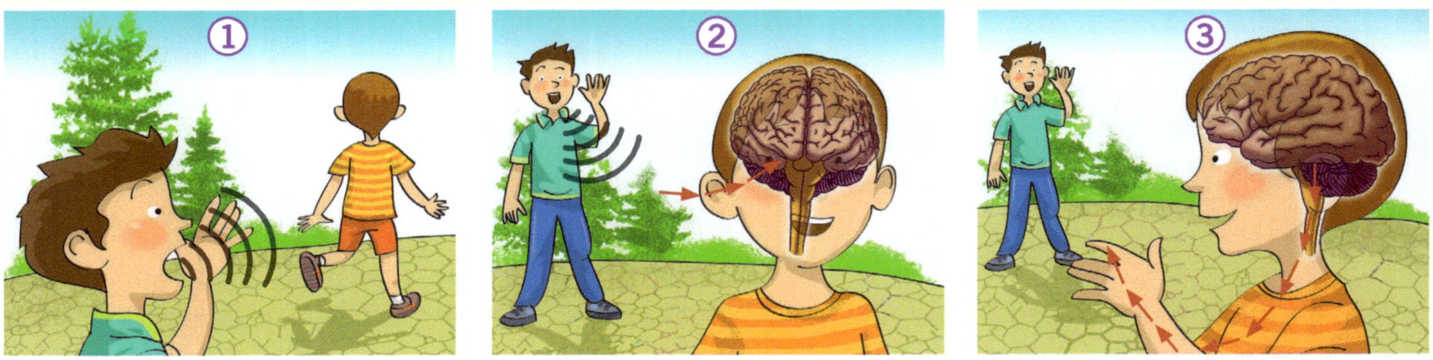

Section
4 The Effects of Alcohol Consumption

Connecting

Alcohol Consumption

The following chart shows the number of times an average adult consumed alcohol in a week between 2005 and 2010.

Alcohol Consumption by Year

Year	Alcohol Consumption (times per week)
2010	6
2009	5
2008	5
2007	3
2006	2
2005	1

1. Think about the information from the table and discuss the questions with your classmates.

a. How much did adult alcohol consumption increase between 2005 and 2010? Interpret

increase → get larger

____

b. What organs do you think are affected by alcohol consumption? Predict

____

One of the most widely consumed drugs is **alcohol**. People who drink alcohol can have serious health problems, including damage to and even cancer of the liver.

As you know, physical activity is a very important part of taking care of our bodies. It is also fundamental to eat a healthy diet and avoid consuming any substance that can damage your body, especially drugs.

Word Focus

Drugs are substances that, when consumed, alter how an organism functions.

Alcoholic drinks are consumed by many people without thinking about the health risks.

Alcoholism

drinks

It is very common to see advertisements for alcoholic beverages that show people having fun and being active. But these advertisements are not real. Consuming alcohol too frequently can damage the body and cause a serious disease called **alcoholism**.

Alcoholism is characterized by an addiction to alcohol. In other words, a person feels the need to drink alcohol too often. This can cause health problems and social problems among families and friends.

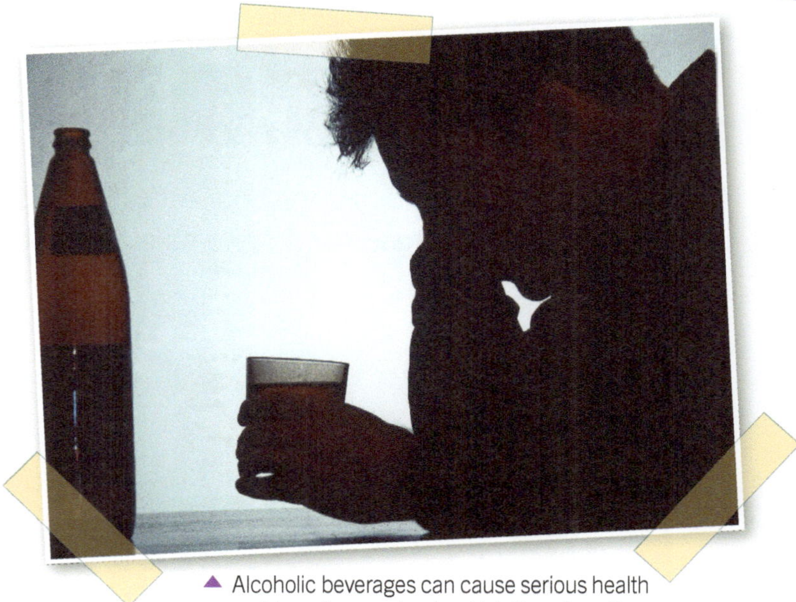

▲ Alcoholic beverages can cause serious health problems for people who drink them too often.

Practicing

2. What is alcoholism? Explain

____

____

____

____

3. How could alcohol affect someone's personal life? Describe

____

____

____

____

Summarizing

Alcohol is a ______________________ and overconsumption of it can cause a disease called ______________________.

Connecting

The Harmful Effects of Alcohol

Alcohol causes changes in how the body functions and can provoke serious problems in different organs and systems of our bodies. For example:

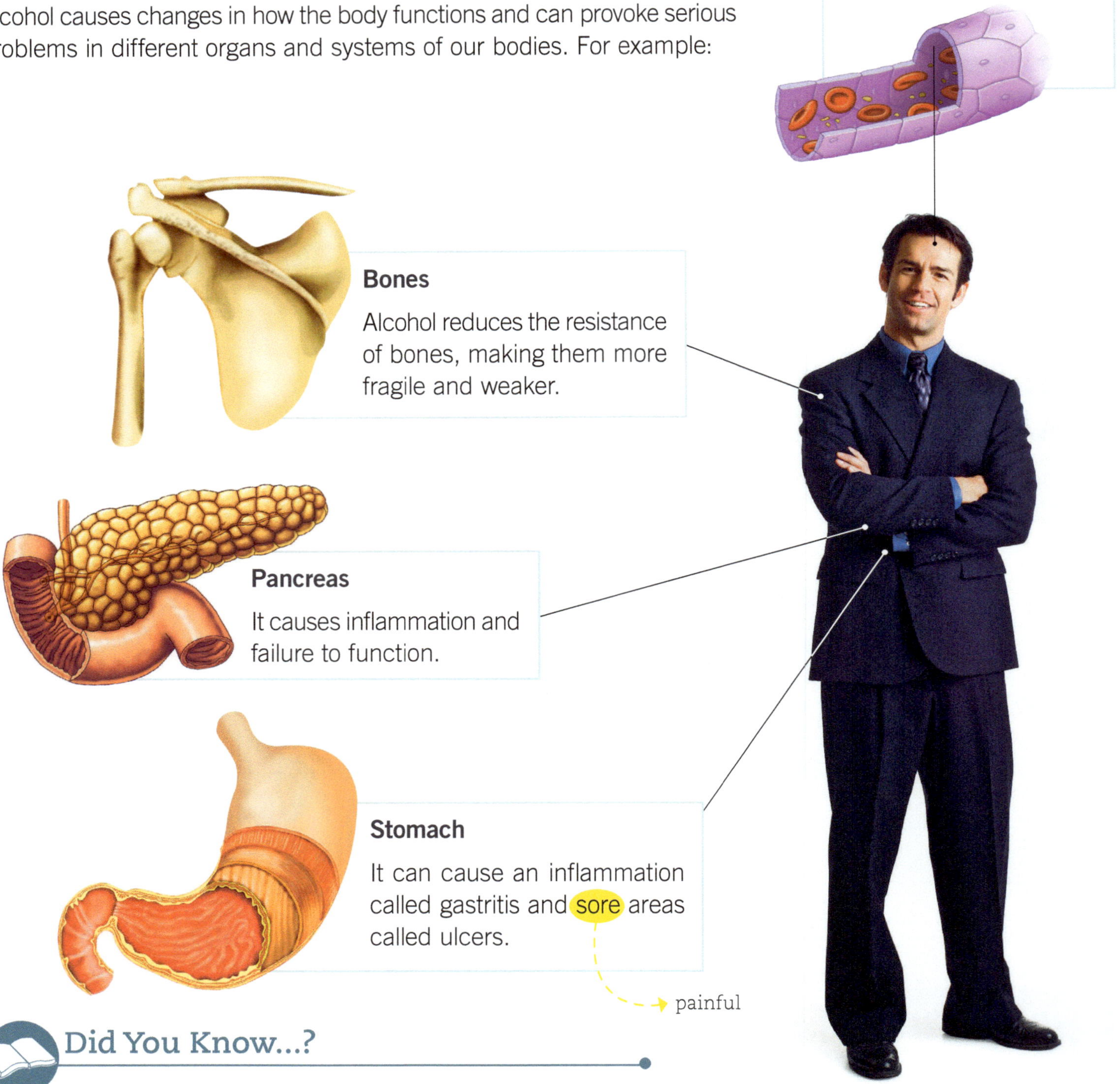

Blood

It causes changes to your blood and circulation.

Bones

Alcohol reduces the resistance of bones, making them more fragile and weaker.

Pancreas

It causes inflammation and failure to function.

Stomach

It can cause an inflammation called gastritis and sore areas called ulcers.

sore → painful

Did You Know...?

Alcohol can also cause problems in people's work relationships as well as with family and friends.

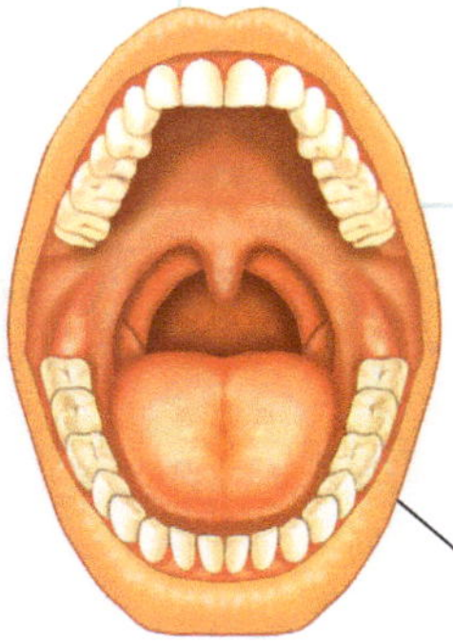

Mouth

It increases the risk of mouth cancer.

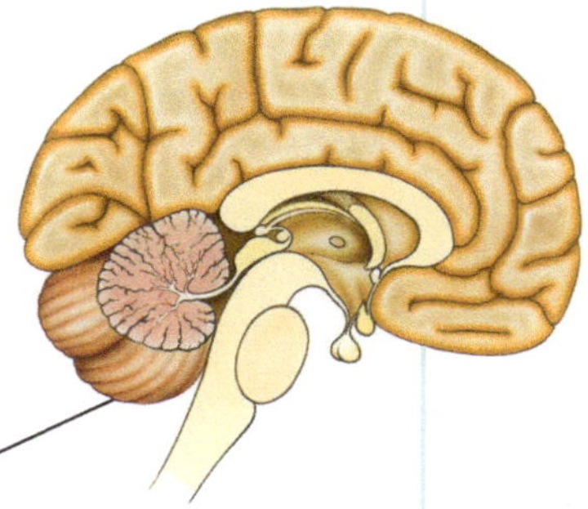

Nervous System

Alcohol affects the brain's normal functions. It causes:

- nausea
- hallucinations
- confusion
- headaches
- body tremors
- lack of coordination
- memory loss

Did You Know...?

Women who drink alcohol while they are pregnant not only cause harm to their own bodies but also to their unborn child. Drinking while pregnant can cause the baby to have serious health problems and **birth defects**.

pregnant: expecting a baby

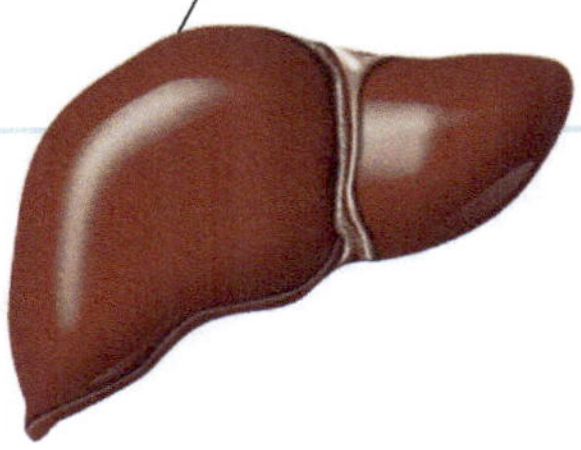

Liver

It hurts the tissue of the liver and causes failure of its normal functions. It can also cause liver cancer.

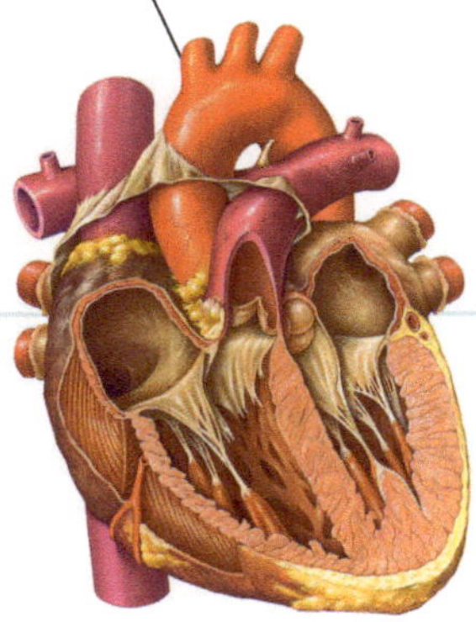

Heart

It causes changes in blood circulation.

Preventing Alcohol Consumption

Since alcohol is a harmful substance, we should avoid consuming it. Here are some ways to do so:

Promote open communication within the family.

Play sports and do exercise in our free time.

Get together with friends to eat and drink healthy products.

Learn about the harmful effects of alcohol.

Practicing

1. Mark each body part that is affected by consuming alcohol with an ✕. Identify

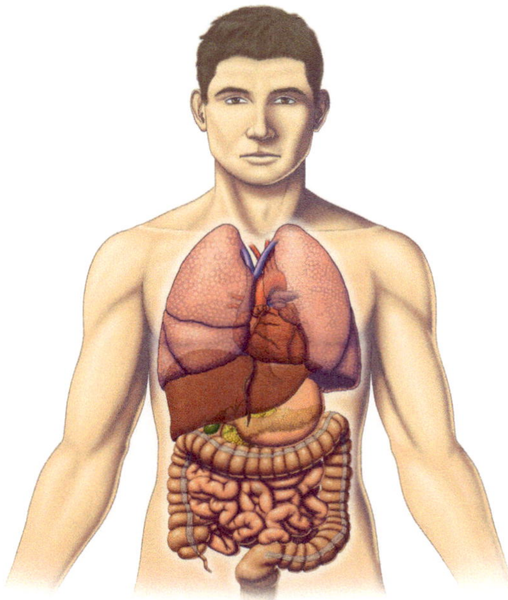

2. What actions are good ways to avoid drinking alcohol? Differentiate

- ☐ Promote open communication within the family.
- ☐ Get informed about the harmful effects of alcohol.
- ☐ Get together with friends to eat and drink healthy products.

Summarizing

Alcoholic drinks can cause serious harm to our ______________________________, so we should avoid consuming them.

Quiz Yourself

1. In groups of three, design a poster about the effects of alcohol on human health.

   The poster should include: making you think

   – An interesting and thought-provoking title.
   – Images that correspond to the subject matter.
   – Three harmful effects of drinking alcohol.
   – A phrase to summarize the information on the poster.

   When you finish, hang the poster up outside your classroom.

What Did You Learn?

1. Go to **Cutout 5** on **page 165** and glue each bone below according to its principal function. Then describe the function.

points
/6

Protection	Support	Movement
______________	______________	______________
______________	______________	______________

2. Move one of your arms as shown in the image.

points
/6

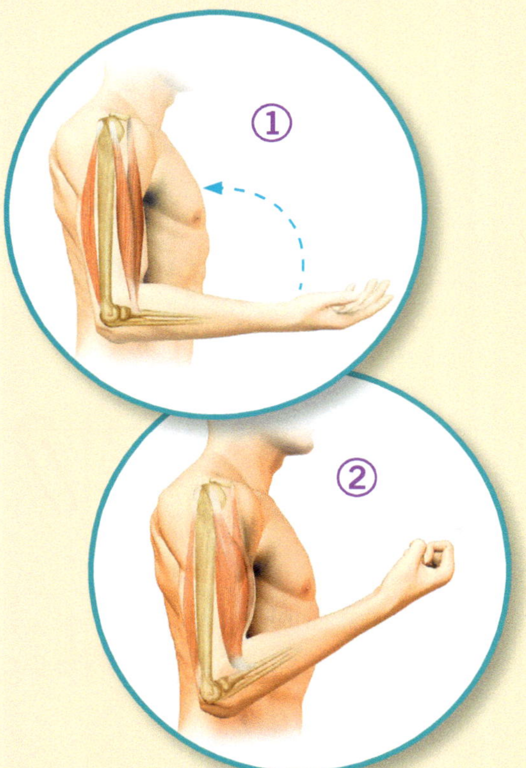

a. Which muscles are used for this action?

____

____

b. Which contract and which expand?

____

____

c. Explain the movement considering the muscles involved and their functions.

____

____

3. Which of the following is **not** a benefit of physical activity? Mark with an ✗.

point
/ 1

A. It makes bones and muscles more resistant.
B. It makes bones and muscles more flexible.
C. It makes bones and muscles more fragile.
D. It makes bones and muscles stronger.

4. Go to **Activity Card 5** and play the memory game. Match each image with its function.

points
/ 5

5. Create a slogan to communicate the negative effects of alcohol to your classmates.

points
/ 2

____
____
____
____

Scientific Skill: Formulate predictions

6. If an adult drinks too much alcohol:

points
/ 4

a. What effects will it have on his or her body? Give an example.

____
____

b. What effects could it have on personal relationships? Give an example.

____
____

Find Test 2 Study Page

Matter

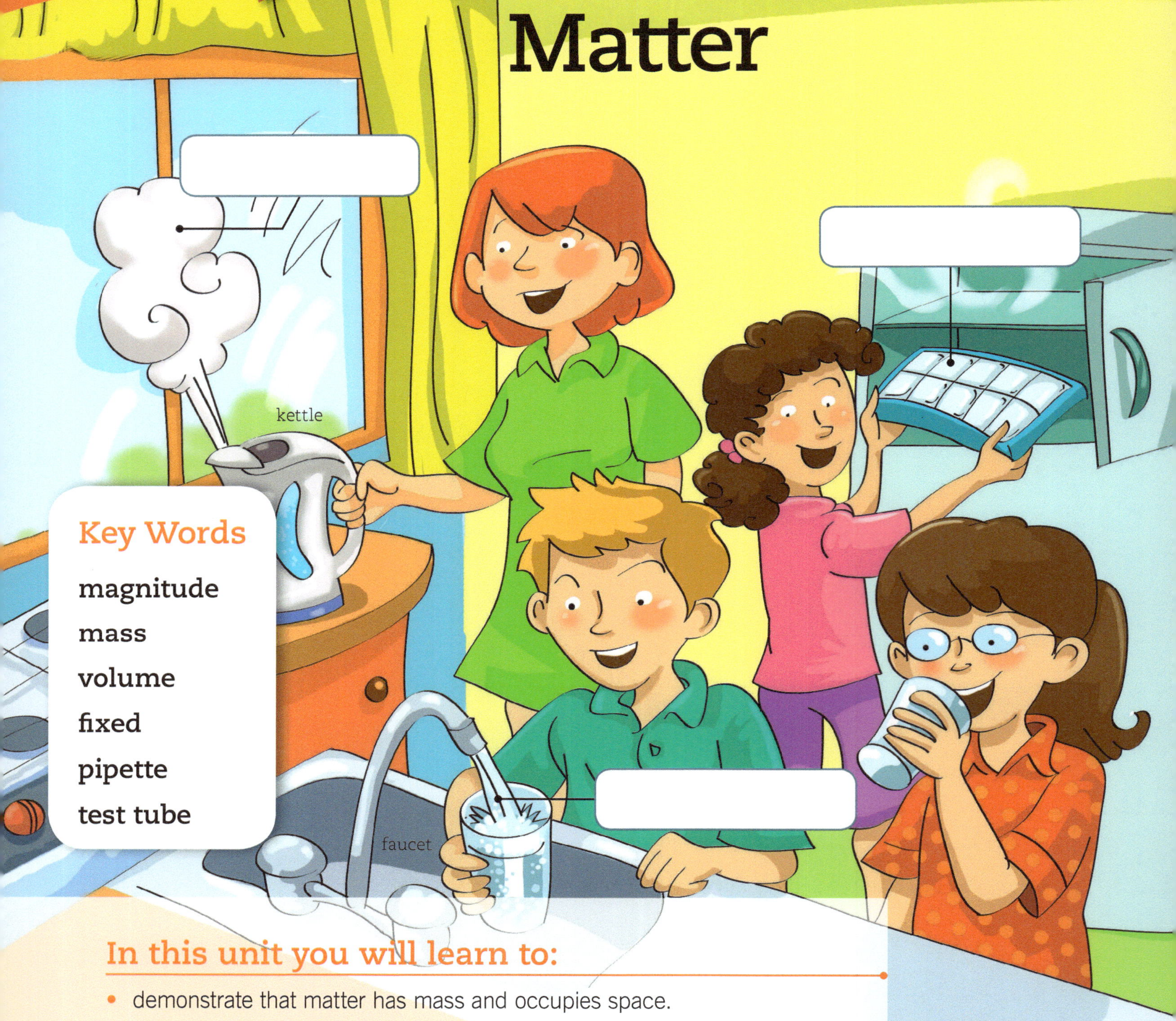

Key Words

magnitude
mass
volume
fixed
pipette
test tube

In this unit you will learn to:

- demonstrate that matter has mass and occupies space.
- compare the physical states of matter.
- measure the mass, volume and temperature of matter using appropriate instruments and units of measurement.
- experiment with changing the state of water.

What Do You Know?

Initial Evaluation

1. Complete the boxes in the picture with the names of the physical states of water.

2. What will happen to the glass of water if it is put into the freezer?

☐ The water will turn into vapor.

☐ The water will turn into ice.

☐ Nothing will change.

Scientific Skill: Experiment

3. What will happen to an ice cube if it is put in sunlight?

a. In which state do you think the ice cube will be at the end of the experiment?

☐ solid ☐ liquid ☐ gas

b. To answer this question, do the following experiment.

- Get an ice cube, a plate and a watch.
- Put the ice cube on the plate.
- Put it in the sun for 30 minutes.
- Observe and record what happens every 10 minutes.

c. What happened to the ice cube after 30 minutes?

☐ It stayed the same. ☐ It became liquid. ☐ It became solid.

d. Which factors do you think caused these changes?

☐ time ☐ temperature ☐ light

Section 1 # Properties of Matter

Connecting

Discovering Matter

1. Look at the scale and answer the following questions. Infer

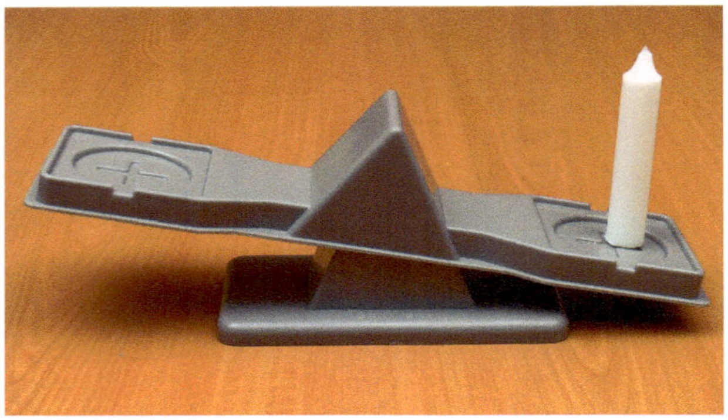

a. What will happen if you place an apple on the empty side?

b. What will happen if you replace the apple with a candle just like the other one?

c. Why do you think that will happen?

2. Look at the sequence of images and respond. Infer

a. What happened when the egg was placed in the cup of water?

____

b. Why do you think that happened?

____

____

c. What would happen if you placed an apple or another object in the cup instead of an egg?

____

____

Practicing

3. Answer the questions according to the examples you have just analyzed.

a. Do all bodies have mass? Infer

____

b. Do all bodies occupy space? Make a drawing to explain your answer. Describe

c. If you compare the candle with the apple, what do they have in common? Compare

____

d. If you know that all bodies consist of matter, how would you define "matter"? Describe

____

____

Summarizing

Matter

has: ______________

occupies: space

Exploring

1. For the following experiment, you need a 20 cm long ruler, something for support (an eraser or small box) and three objects: an eraser, a pencil sharpener and a paper clip.

Experiment

- Place the ruler on top of the support that you chose, as in the image.
- Take two objects and put one on each side of the ruler. Observe what happens.

a. Repeat the experiment with each pair of objects and complete the table.

Objects	Toward Which Object Does the Balance Scale Tilt?
eraser and sharpener	
eraser and clip	
clip and sharpener	

b. Do all objects have mass? How do you know?

____

c. Is mass the same in all objects?

____

d. How would you explain what mass is?

____

Mass is the amount of matter that a body has. Mass does not vary. It is always the same no matter where the body is located or what conditions it is in. Mass is measured with an instrument called a **scale**. Its unit of measurement is the **kilogram (kg)**. Small bodies such as rice can also be measured in **grams (g),** and large bodies like ships can be measured in **tons (t)**.

Practicing

2. Does air have mass? Prove it! You need a thin ruler or a thin wooden stick approximately 30 cm long, two balloons of the same size and three pieces of string of equal length. Predict

- Blow up the balloons, making sure that they are both the same size, and tie each to a piece of string.
- Tie the third piece of string to the middle of the ruler or stick.
- Take the ruler and tie one balloon to each end.
- Balance them as you see in the image.

inflate

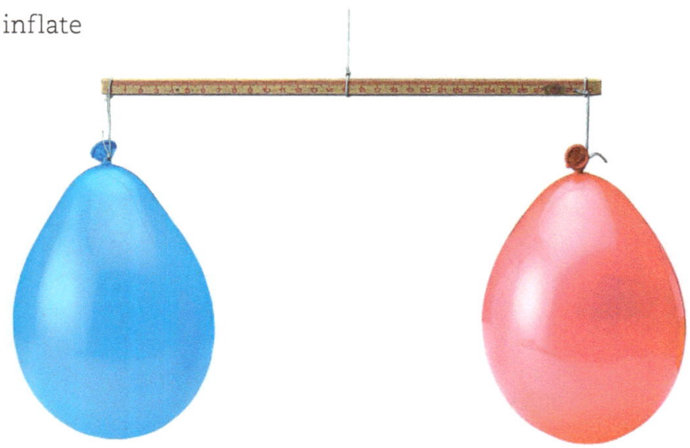

Tip

Mass is not the same as weight. **Mass** is the amount of matter. **Weight** is the measurement of the pull of gravity on a body.

a. What is the mass of the balloons? ______________________

b. Ask your teacher to carefully pop a balloon and observe. What happened when the balloon was popped?

____

c. Which balloon has the greater mass now? Why?

____

____

d. Could you say that air has mass? How is this demonstrated in this experiment?

____

____

Summarizing

Mass corresponds to the ______________ of matter. This is measured with a ______________,

and its unit of measurement is the ______________________.

Exploring

Volume

1. To do the following experiment, you need an eraser, a potato, a metal pencil sharpener, three plastic plates, three transparent plastic cups of the same size and water. Predict

- Fill the cups with water and place them on the plates, as you see in the image.

- Put an object in each cup (the eraser, potato or sharpener).
- Look at the volume of water that each object has displaced. Pay attention to the water that spilled onto the plate.

go under water

overflowed

a. Why does water spill out when an object is submerged into a cup full of water?

____

b. Why do some objects displace more water than other objects?

____

c. How could you define the concept of volume?

____

d. Can two objects occupy the same space at the same time? Explain.

____

The **space that a body occupies** is called **volume**. Depending on the state that the body is in, volume may or may not vary. The volume of a liquid can be measured with various instruments, but the most commonly used are graduated cylinders, flasks and **pipettes**. The unit of measurement for volume is the **cubic centimeter (cm^3)**, but we usually use **liters (l)** or **milliliters (ml)**.

Practicing

2. Which object has more volume? Mark with a ✔. Identify

clip

die

sphere

3. Put some paper at the bottom of a plastic cup. Next, fill a bowl with water. Dip the cup into the bowl as shown in the image. Observe what happens. Infer

a. Why did the paper not become wet?

____

____

____

____

b. What is in the cup that prevents the water from entering?

____

c. What could you do to let the water enter?

____

d. Do you think that air has volume? Explain.

____

Summarizing

Volume is ______________________________.

Some of its units of measurement are ______________________________.

Connecting

Matter

1. Look at the following pictures and answer according to what you have studied on the previous pages.
Compare and contrast

a. What do the rhinoceros and the plant have in common? How are they different?

Similarities	Differences

b. Compare the rhinoceros with the cushion and pebbles. Do they have the same amount of mass? Explain.

____

c. Compare the plant with the soap and the feather. Do they occupy the same volume? Explain.

____

Even though the objects are different in shape, size, color, taste or texture, they are all composed of matter. **Matter** is everything that has **mass** and occupies space or, in other words, has **volume**. Mass and volume are **properties of matter**.

Practicing

2. Explain why an elephant and a ball consist of matter. Draw a picture to help you. Explain

____

____

____

____

Summarizing

Matter is everything that has ______________________________.

Quiz Yourself

1. Use an experiment to demonstrate a property of matter. Write and draw the activity that you will do.

What do you need?

____

____

What do you have to do?

____

____

Results:

____

____

Conclusion:

____

____

Section 2

Physical States of Matter

Connecting

Solids, Liquids and Gases

1. Look at the following images and discuss the questions with your classmates. Apply

▲ ladybug

▲ drops of water

▲ stove flame

a. What do these images have in common?
b. Is everything in the images matter?
c. What physical state are they in?

As you know, everything around us is matter. Matter has mass and occupies space, but what is matter?

- Matter consists of **particles**.
- Particles are always in movement or vibrating.
- Between particles, there are forces that allow them to stay together and apart.
- Some of the states in which matter can exist are **solid**, **liquid** or **gas**.

To understand how matter can be found in different states, we must take into account the force of attraction between its particles.

tightly: very closely, densely

Solids	Liquids	Gas
The particles are tightly packed and are in **fixed** positions, which is why they vibrate and do not move.	The particles are packed together but not rigidly like in solids. They have more space between them, which means they can move around.	The particles are completely separated from each other and can move around freely. There is no force that keeps the particles together.
	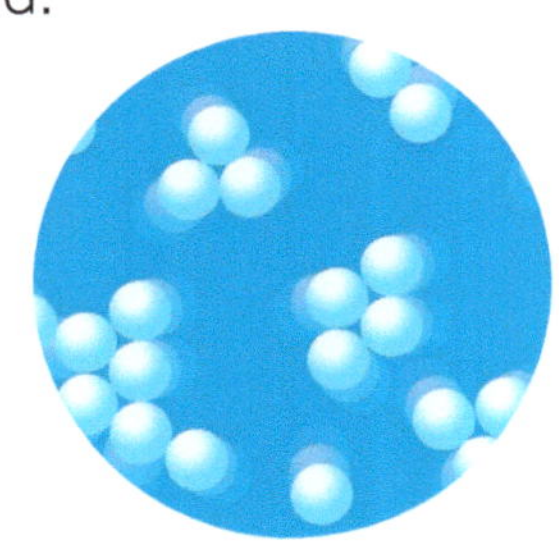	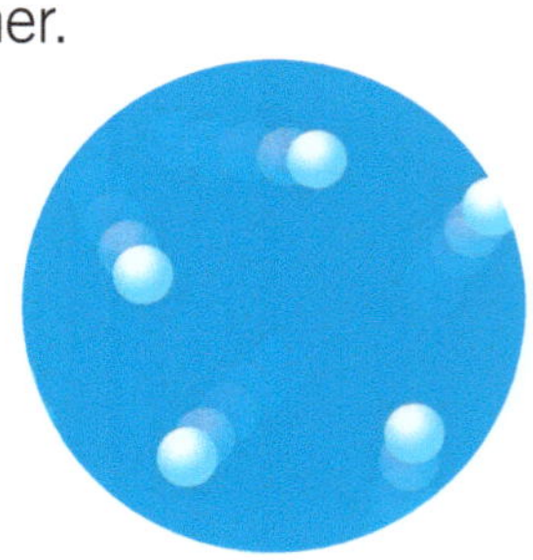

Practicing

2. Look around you and write some examples of matter found in the following states.

Solid	Liquid	Gas

a. Which state was the easiest to find? Why?

____

3. Find in the image examples of each state of matter. Identify

Solid: ______________________________

Liquid: ______________________________

Gas: ______________________________

Summarizing

Matter can be found in a state of
- ______________________________
- ______________________________
- ______________________________

Exploring

Matter Has Shape and Volume

What shape and volume does matter have? To answer this question, do the following experiment.

1. For the following experiment, you will need an eraser, water and three different containers, such as a plastic cup, a test tube and a plastic plate. To analyze this experiment, complete the report on **Activity Cards 6** and **7**.
   Experiment

Did You Know...?

Most gases are colorless because the particles are so far apart from each other.

colorless: with no color

Experiment 1

- Take the test tube and fill it with water.
- Pour the water into the plastic cup.
- Finally, pour the same water onto the plastic plate.

Be careful while working with the test tube because it is made of glass.

Experiment 2

- Take the eraser and put it into the test tube. Does it fit?
- Put the same eraser into the plastic cup.
- Finally, put the eraser on the plastic plate.

Remember to clean up after yourself when you have finished the activity.

The particles of liquids are more separated than the particles in solids. They also move around easily, which means that they can move on top of and around each other. As a result, liquids adopt the shape of their container—in other words, they **do not have a fixed shape**. The particles of solid matter are tightly packed together, so they are difficult to separate. This explains why solids have a **fixed shape**. However, the volume of solids and liquids does not change; therefore, both solids and liquids have a **constant volume**.

fixed: unchanging

Gas occupies all the available space; therefore, its **volume is not constant**. This also means **it does not have a fixed shape**, but it takes the shape of the container it is in.

Education through Values

The most abundant liquid on earth is water. However, fresh water is necessary for life and it is very **scarce**. Always remember not to waste or pollute water. In this way, you will be helping the environment.

Practicing

2. Look at the following image and answer. Analyze

a. Do you think that the representation of the particles is correct? Explain.

____

____

____

____

3. Look at the image and answer. Predict

a. How are the particles distributed inside the balloon? Draw them in the image.

b. If you let the air out, what shape will the air take?

____

____

c. When you let the air out of the balloon, will it have the same volume?

____

____

d. Does air have a fixed shape?

____

____

Summarizing

Solids have a ____________________ shape and ____________________ volume.

Liquids adapt to ______________________________ and have __________ volume.

____________ do not have a definite shape or constant volume.

Exploring

Matter Flows

lift or elevate one side

1. Collect a plastic tray, a cup of water, an eraser and some paper towels. Tilt the tray. You can put a support under the tilted side.
   - Place the eraser on the side that is elevated and watch what happens.
   - Next, in the same place you put the eraser, slowly add some water and watch what happens.

a. What happened with the eraser? Explain

____

b. What happened with the water? Explain

____

c. Which one has the ability to **flow**? Infer

____

d. What would happen if a gas were used instead of water? Predict

____

Liquids have the **ability to flow**. To flow means to move in a stream from one place to another because the forces uniting the particles are weak. **Gas** also has the ability to flow, since it has almost no forces keeping it together.

Solids, on the contrary, **do not have the ability to flow**. The force that unites their particles is very strong.

Staying Healthy

When you do an experiment, you must never taste or smell the materials that you use as they could be toxic.

Word Focus

Flow is the ability of liquids to continuously move from one place to another.

Practicing

2. Collect a spoon, a tray and four plastic cups. Fill each cup halfway with one of the following materials: liquid soap, salt, lentils or oil.

- Observe their shape, color and transparency. Move the cups slowly so they do not spill.

a. How are they similar? How are they different? Compare and contrast

____

____

- Tilt the tray. Then place a spoonful of each material at the top of the tray and observe.

b. Which elements were able to flow? Apply

____

c. How is the behavior of the materials similar to water? Explain

____

____

d. If you could add gas to a cup, how would it behave? Predict

____

____

Summarizing

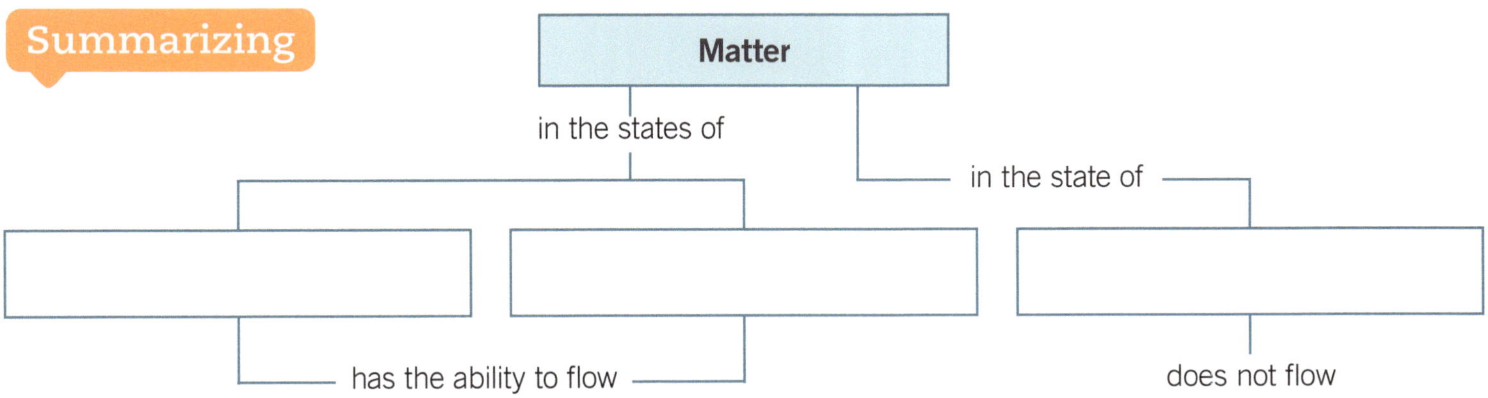

Exploring

Matter Expands and Compresses

1. To do this activity, you need a syringe without a needle, water and crushed ice.

   - Pick up the syringe and lift the plunger halfway so that you fill the syringe with air. Block the end of the syringe with your finger and push the plunger down. Observe what happens.

   a. Does the volume of air increase, decrease or remain the same? Identify

   plunger → the movable part of a syringe

   ____

   - Next, keeping your finger on the end of the syringe, pull the plunger again and observe what happens.

   b. Does the volume of air increase, decrease or remain the same? Identify

   ____

   c. What would happen if you did the same experiment with water? Predict

   ____

   d. What would happen if you did the same experiment with crushed ice? Predict

   ____

   e. What conclusion can you make? Conclude

   ____

   ____

   ____

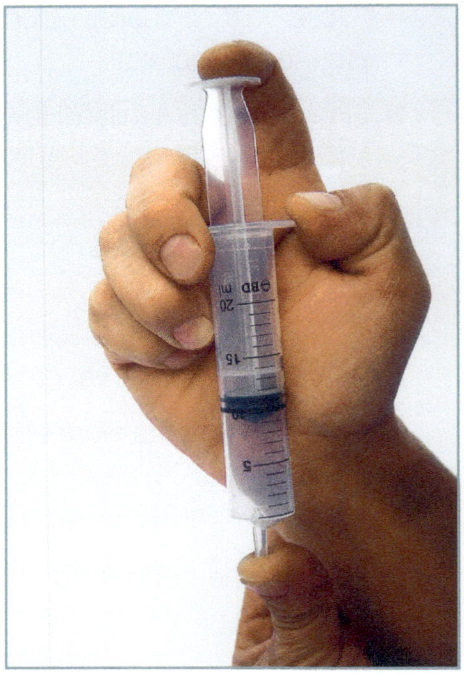

Matter in **its gas state compresses**. This means it can decrease in volume if force is applied to it. But if the container increases in volume, the gas **expands**. In other words, gases can occupy all the space available. Matter in a **solid or liquid state does not compress or expand**.

Did You Know...?

A diver's tank contains the same volume of air as a small room. The difference is that the air in the tank is compressed.

Practicing

2. Fill two balloons with the same amount of air. Make sure that they have the same volume. Infer

- Place one of the balloons inside a freezer for ten minutes.
- After ten minutes, take the balloon out and compare it to the other balloon, as you see in the image.

a. What happened to the particles of air inside the balloon?

____

____

b. What properties of gas does this experiment demonstrate?

____

____

▲ Balloons, after one was in a freezer for 10 minutes.

3. Read the description and answer. Infer

Kristine's mother sprayed a room with air freshener. Kristine was in another room, but she could still smell the aroma.

a. Why could Kristine smell the aroma while in another room?

____

____

b. What properties of gas can we observe in this case?

____

____

Challenge

Can you say that gas flows like a liquid? Why or why not?

Summarizing

Gases can ____________________ and ____________________; however, ____________________ and ____________________ cannot.

Connecting

Changing States of Matter

1. When Barbara got back from school, it was very hot, so her mother bought her an ice cream. Her friend Cameron invited her to play, and she put the ice cream on a plate. After 15 minutes, she returned and found her ice cream had melted. Identify

- Discuss with your classmates.

a. What happened to the ice cream?

b. Which state was the ice cream in when her mother bought it? Which state was it in after 15 minutes?

c. What caused this change in the ice cream?

When matter changes from one physical form to another, a **change in state** occurs. Changes of state happen when there is an **increase** or a **decrease in temperature**.

Melting or Fusion: change from a solid state to a liquid state because of an increase in temperature.

Vaporization: change from a liquid state to a gas state, generally because of an increase in temperature.

Deposition: change from a gas state to a solid state because of a decrease in temperature.

Solidification: change from a liquid state to a solid state because of a decrease in temperature.

Condensation: change from a gas state to a liquid state because of a decrease in temperature.

Sublimation: change from a solid state to a gas state because of an increase in temperature.

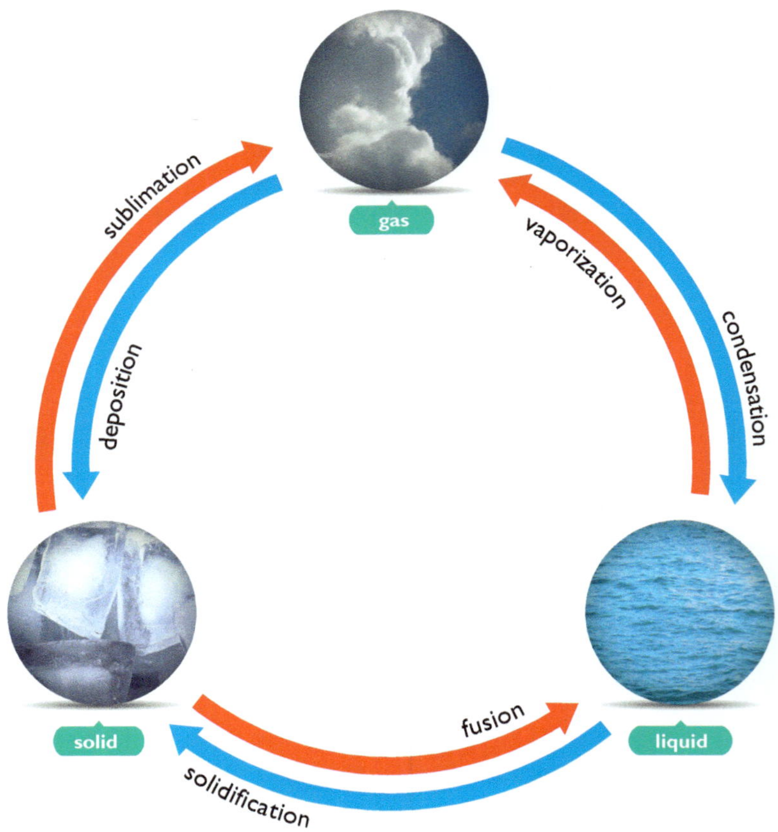

Practicing

2. Write three different examples of a change in state.

- ______________________________
- ______________________________
- ______________________________

Summarizing

Matter changes from one physical state to another as a result of a ______________________ in ______________________. These changes are called ______________________.

Quiz Yourself

1. Complete the table.

	Apple	Air	Milk
Does it maintain its shape?			
Is its volume constant?			
Does it adapt to its container?			
Does it flow?			
Can it be compressed?			
Can it expand?			
How close are the particles?			

2. Can the water in a river change its state? Explain how.

____

____

Let's Check!

1. Write the letter of each concept next to the corresponding definition.

points
/8

A Mass	☐	Space that a body uses.
B Gas	☐	Everything that has mass and occupies space.
C Matter	☐	The amount of matter that a body has.
D Flow	☐	The ability to decrease its volume when force is applied.
E Volume	☐	The ability to move continuously from one place to another.
F Liquid	☐	Its particles are tightly packed together and in fixed positions.
G Compression	☐	Its particles are packed together firmly but not rigidly.
H Solid	☐	Its particles are completely separated and can move freely.

2. Go to **Cutout 6** on **page 165**. Glue the image that best represents the particles of the notebook. Think about what state of matter it is in.

points
/2

3. Go to **Cutout 7** on **page 167**. Glue the images in order according to the characteristics of the particles.

points
/ 9

a. The force of attraction between the particles from the strongest to the weakest.

b. The distance between the particles from the greatest to the least.

c. The movement between the particles from the most to the least.

4. What change in state occurs in each of the following situations?

points
/ 4

a. The drops of water that form on a cool window. ____________________

b. A melting ice cube. ____________________

c. Clothes drying in sunlight. ____________________

d. Water in an ice tray transforming into ice. ____________________

Section
3 Measuring Matter

Exploring

Measuring the Properties of Matter

How tall are you? When you buy a soda, how do you ask for it? You may have heard these questions more than once, and their answers usually include a number with a unit of measurement. How do you know it is the appropriate unit of measurement? Here, you will learn about magnitudes and their corresponding units of measurement. You will also learn the instruments that are used to measure them.

Word Focus

Magnitudes are properties that can be measured and expressed with a number and a unit of measurement.

Measuring Mass

To measure mass, we use an instrument called a scale, which can come in various shapes and sizes. The unit of measurement for mass is the **kilogram (kg)**. It is also common to use grams (g) or tons (t). A ton is equivalent to 1,000 kg.

▲ electronic scale

1. We are going to learn to measure the mass of different objects. To do this, you need an electronic scale and four different objects, such as a notebook, a cup, a ruler and an eraser. Measure

- Make sure that the scale is placed on a surface that does not move.
- Look at the scale and make sure it reads 0.
- Put an object on the scale.
- Look at the scale and record the value that it shows. Always write the unit of measurement!
- Repeat the procedure for each object.

a. Complete the table.

Object	Mass	Unit

▲ balance scale with two plates

Measuring Volume

There are various methods to find the volume of a body. The method to use depends on the physical state of the object that is being studied. First, you will learn how to measure the volume of a liquid.

Some instruments that we use to measure volume are graduated cylinders, pipettes, flasks and burettes. The unit of measurement that we use for liquids is the liter (l), which is equivalent to 1,000 milliliters (ml).

▲ graduated cylinder and pipette

2. You are going to learn how to measure the volume of a liquid. In this case, you will measure 50 ml. You will need a pitcher of water, a plastic cup, a dropper and a 100 ml graduated cylinder. Measure

- Make sure that the cylinder is on a surface that does not move.
- Put some water into the cup, and then slowly start emptying it into the cylinder.
- Fill the cylinder with 48 ml of water.
- Use the dropper to add water until you reach 50 ml.
- Make sure that the lowest part of the **meniscus** of the water sits on the 50 ml line, as shown in the illustration.

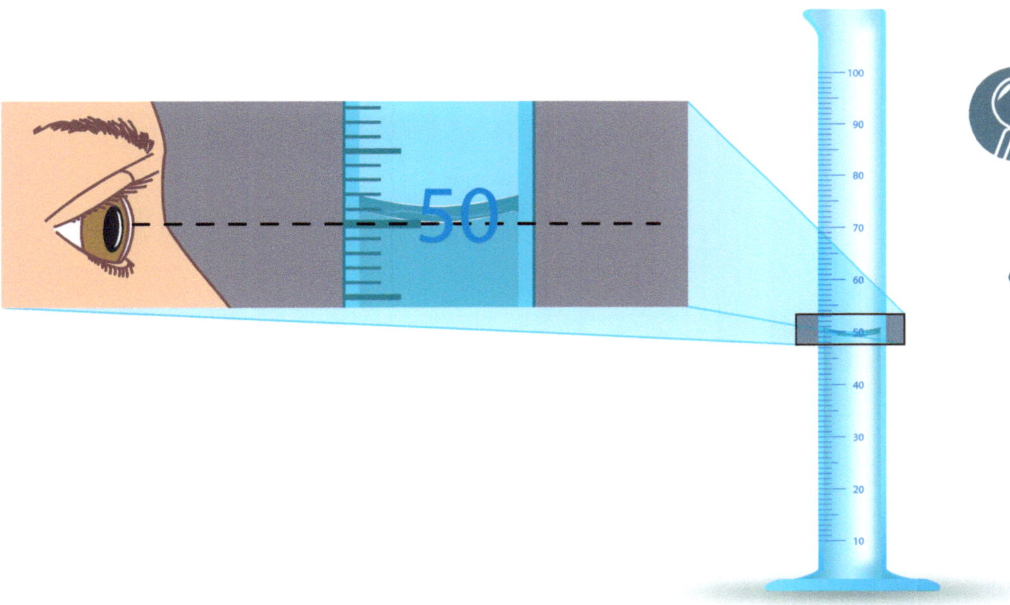

Word Focus

The **meniscus** is the curved upper surface of a liquid.

a. Why do you think it is necessary to add water with a dropper from the 48 ml line to reach the 50 ml line?

___

___

Measuring Temperature

Temperature is a magnitude that gives information about the movement of the particles in a body. To measure temperature, an instrument called a **thermometer** is used. Thermometers can use different scales, such as the **Kelvin scale (K)** and the **Celsius scale (°C)**.

3. You will learn how to measure the temperature of water. Collect three Styrofoam cups, an alcohol thermometer, ice, warm water, room-temperature water, a retort stand and clamps. Measure

- Put the equipment together as you see in the image.
- Pour the room-temperature water into one of the cups.
- Place it under the retort stand.
- Lower the thermometer into the water. Caution: the thermometer must not touch the sides of the cup.
- Wait a few minutes and write down the temperature displayed on the thermometer.
- Repeat this procedure with the ice and warm water.

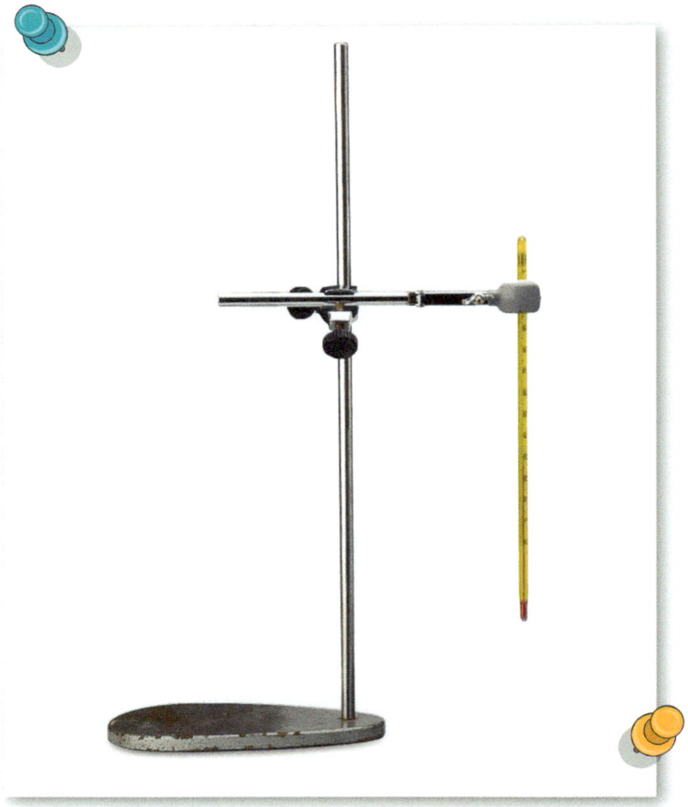

a. Complete the table and answer.

	Ice	Room-temperature Water	Warm Water
Temperature			
Unit of Measurement			

b. Which of the three cups has the highest temperature? ______________________

c. Which has the lowest temperature? ______________________

d. What unit of measurement did you use to measure the temperature? ______________________

Practicing

4. Match the laboratory instruments with the magnitudes. Then match them with the corresponding unit of measurement. Identify

scale	volume	degrees Celsius
cylinder	temperature	grams
thermometer	mass	liters

Summarizing

Magnitude	Unit of Measurement	Symbol of Unit of Measurement	Measuring Instrument
Volume			
Mass			
Temperature			

Quiz Yourself

1. Explain how you would measure the mass, volume and temperature of a glass of milk. Which instruments and units of measurement could you use?

Science Lab

Does Making Ice Pops Produce a Change in State?

Basic Framework

There are many ways to demonstrate that a body consists of matter, has mass and changes its state. To prove this, we will make ice pops.

Observation

Which of these ingredients can change their physical states? Circle them.

oil

salt

water

juice powder

butter

Research Question

When you make ice pops, is there a change in physical state?

Hypothesis

The water will transform into ice if you put it in a freezer.

Prediction

Mark your prediction.

☐ The water will change into ice when you put it in a freezer.

☐ The water will evaporate when you put it in a freezer.

Experimental Procedure

1. Form groups of five and collect the following materials:

- water
- 1 liter graduated cylinder
- a scale
- 5 ice cream sticks
- juice powder
- a pitcher
- 5 plastic cups
- a mixing rod or a spoon

2. Place a piece of clean paper on the scale. On top of this, add the juice powder. Measure its mass and record it.
3. Use the cylinder to pour 1 liter of water into the pitcher.
4. Pour the juice powder into the pitcher of water. Stir.
5. Pour 100 ml of juice into each cup. Use the cylinder to do this.
6. Put an ice cream stick into each cup, and then put the cups in a freezer for one hour.

Experimenting is a practical way of testing and examining an object or a phenomenon.

Results

1. Record the data.
   a. Mass of the juice powder. ______________________
   b. Volume of the water. ______________________
   c. Physical state of the water and juice mix at the beginning of the activity. ______________________
   d. Physical state of the water and juice mix at the end of the activity. ______________________

Interpreting and Analyzing the Results

1. Which instrument allowed you to measure the juice powder's mass?

____

2. Which instrument allowed you to measure the water's volume?

____

3. Which factor produced the change in state?

____

Conclusions

1. Is there a change in state when you make an ice pop? Explain.

____

____

____

What Did You Learn?

1. How would you explain to somebody that a ball is matter? Explain.

points
/ 2

____

____

2. Complete the table.

points
/ 24

	Solid	Liquid	Gas
Draw the particles.			
Does it maintain its shape?			
Does it have constant volume?			
Can it easily adapt to the container it is in?			
Can it flow?			
Can it be compressed?			
Can it expand?			
How separated are the particles?			

3. In what state are an ice cube and the air inside a balloon, respectively? Mark the correct answer with a ✔.

point
/ 1

A. Gas – gas.

B. Liquid – gas.

C. Solid – gas.

D. Solid – solid.

Final Evaluation

4. Describe the procedure that you would use to measure the mass and volume of a clay sphere.

points ___ / 4

a. Procedure to measure mass:

____

____

b. Procedure to measure volume:

____

____

____

Scientific Skill: Experiment

5. Does the mass of a body change when its state changes?

points ___ / 6

- Add 150 ml of warm water to a beaker and add some ice cubes.
- Cover the beaker with plastic wrap so that it is completely sealed.
- Immediately measure the beaker's mass and write it in the table under initial mass.
- Wait a few minutes until the ice melts, and then measure the mass again. Write the results in the table under final mass.

Initial Mass	Final Mass

a. Did the mass vary when the ice changed state? Explain.

____

b. Would we get the same result if we did not cover the beaker? Explain.

____

____

Find Test 3 Study Page

Unit 4

Force and Motion

Key Words

trajectory

displacement

attract

repel

weight

interact

In this unit you will learn to:

- identify the principal measurements of motion.
- demonstrate the effects of force on objects.
- identify different types of forces and their effects.
- build objects that show the effects of force.
- compare predictions with observations when building a spring scale.

What Do You Know?

Initial Evaluation

1. Circle the situations that show some type of force in [orange].
2. Circle the situations that show movements in [green].
3. What do you think the bridge is made out of? Why?

___

___

Scientific Skill: Compare and contrast

4. Do the following activities.

   a. What would happen if you put a ball of paper in front of a fan? Make a prediction.

   ___

   ___

   b. Make a small ball out of paper. Put it on the table and blow on it, as you see in the photograph.

   c. What happens? Record your results.

   ___

   ___

   d. Compare your prediction with your observations. Was your prediction correct? Explain.

   ___

   ___

Section
1 Motion

Connecting

Trajectory and Displacement

As you can see all around, **motion** is a part of everyday life, such as when you ride a bicycle or fly a kite. Motion is defined as the **change in position of a body** or, in other words, when a body changes its location with respect to a point of reference. But is it possible to study motion? Yes! In order to study motion, it is necessary to know more about certain concepts like **trajectory** and **displacement**.

Remember!

A **body** is an object or the physical self of an animal or human.

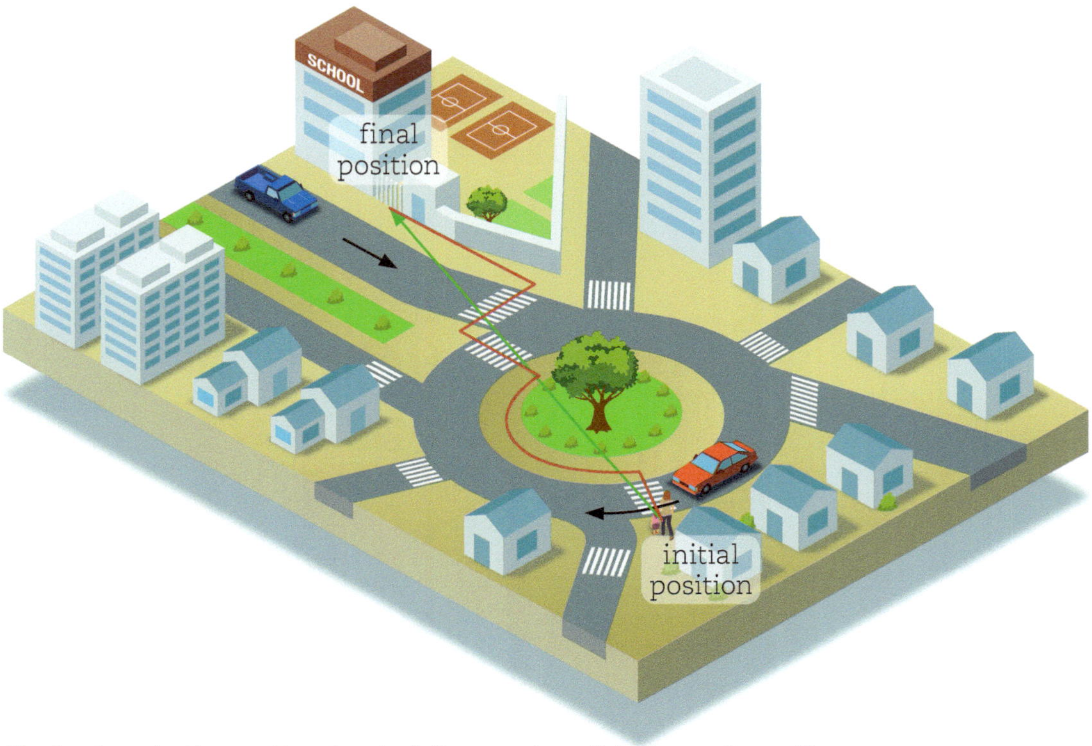

The red line represents the trajectory. The green arrow represents the displacement.

Trajectory is the path a body follows when it is in motion. If you measure the length of the trajectory, you will know the **distance traveled**.

In the image above, you see a girl walking with her mom to her school. Is the indicated trajectory (the red line) the only path they can take? The answer is no because there are many possible trajectories. If you want to go from one place to another, there are usually many pathways. Trajectory can also be a **straight line**, like the path of the blue truck, or **curved**, like the path of the red car.

Another important concept is **displacement**, which is shown by the green arrow in the picture that connects the initial position of a body's movement to the final position.

The amount of distance traveled (the length of the trajectory) and the displacement can be the same if a body travels in a straight line.

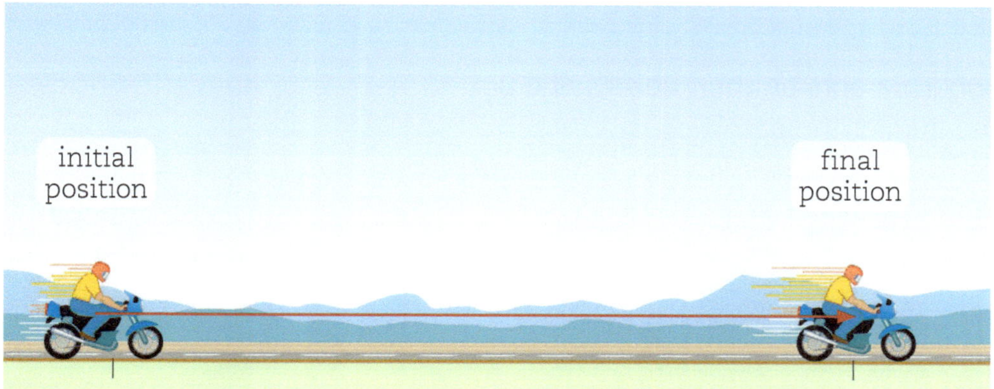

◀ The red line represents the distance traveled. The red arrow represents the displacement. In this case, the two are the same.

Practicing

1. In the image:

a. Draw the trajectory in [red] and the displacement with an arrow in [blue]. Apply

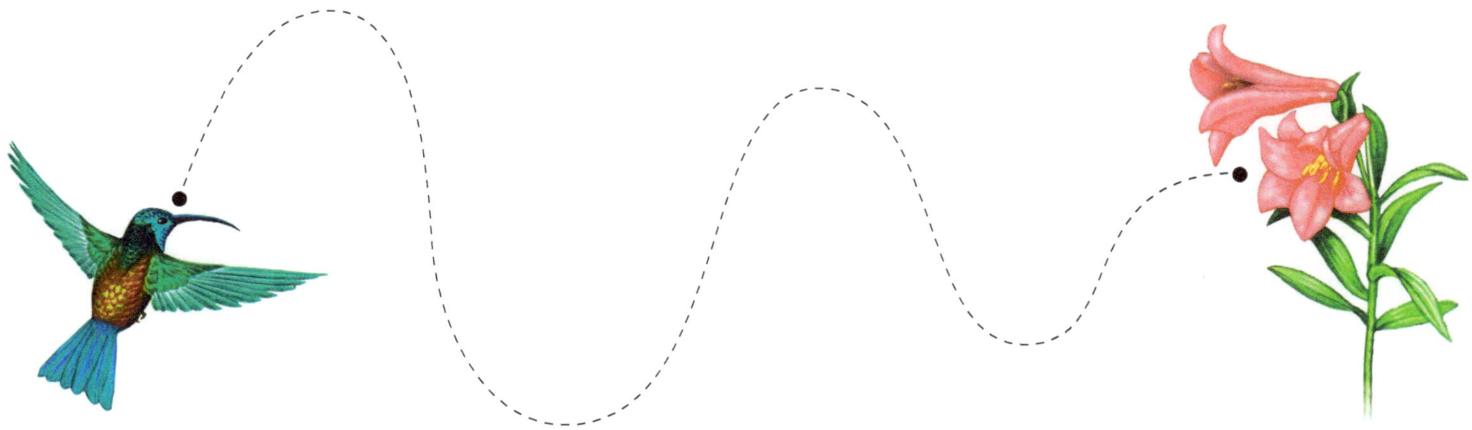

b. Is the distance traveled equal to the displacement? Explain. Compare and contrast

____

Summarizing

The trajectory is the _______________________ by a moving body.

Displacement is the arrow that connects the _______________________ to the _______________________ of a body's movement.

Connecting

Speed

Imagine you are riding in a car with your parents on the freeway, and a train is passing by. Which is faster, the train or the car?

Speed is related to the distance a body travels during a determined amount of time. Generally, a train travels a greater distance in less time than a car, so its speed is greater.

Just like mass and volume, speed also has a corresponding unit of measurement. The most common is **kilometers per hour**, which is represented as **km/h**. It can also be expressed in meters per second (m/s).

Fun Fact!

The word **velocity** is normally used to refer to the speed of a body. However, unlike speed, velocity measures both the speed and **direction** of the motion of an object, like horizontal, vertical, diagonal, up, down, left or right.

The cheetah is one of the **fastest** animals on the planet. It can run up to 114 km/h when chasing its prey!

Calculating the Speed of an Object

How can we calculate the speed at which an object travels? Well, speed corresponds to the relationship between distance traveled and time taken.

Speed can be calculated using the following equation:

$$\text{speed} = \frac{\text{distance}}{\text{time}}$$

Let's analyze the following example: Robbie walked 8 meters in 4 seconds.

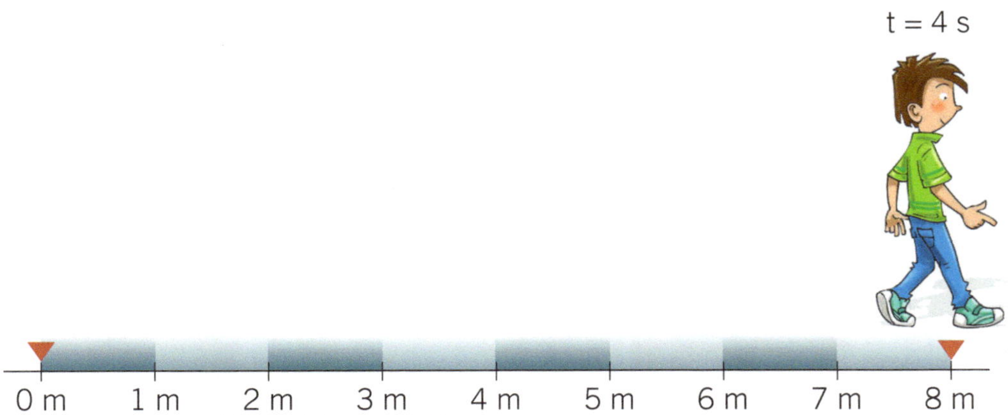

At what speed did Robbie walk?

First, write down the data from the problem.

Distance: 8 meters
Time: 4 seconds

Then write the equation to calculate speed.

$$\text{speed} = \frac{\text{distance}}{\text{time}}$$

Next, put the data into the speed equation.

$$\text{speed} = \frac{8}{4}$$

Finally, calculate and write the answer to the division equation.

$$\text{speed} \longrightarrow 8 \div 4 = 2$$

Therefore, Robbie walked at a speed of 2 m/s.

Did You Know...?

Speed in the air or water is measured in **knots**.

Do not forget to write the speed with its unit of measurement. In this case, speed is expressed in m/s because the distance was measured in meters and the time in seconds.

Practicing

1. Look at the following image. Apply

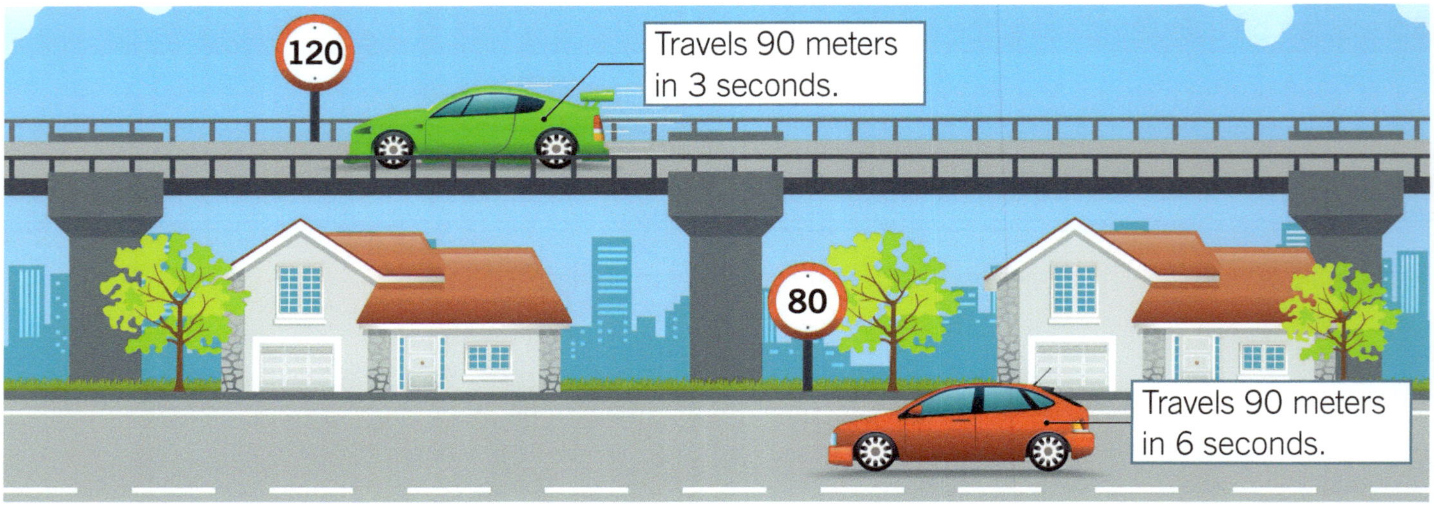

a. Complete the table.

	Car 1 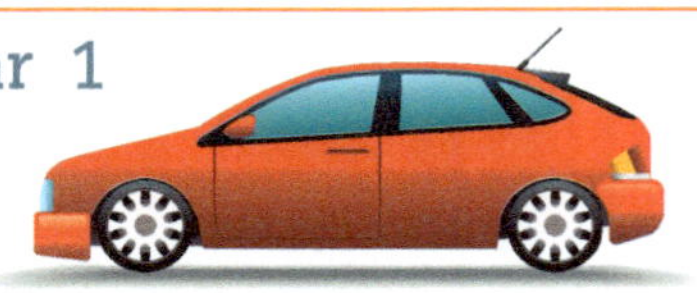	Car 2 
Distance (meters)		
Time (seconds)		
Speed		

b. Which car is **faster**? ______________________________

c. How can the speed of an object be expressed? Explain using an example.

____

____

Summarizing

Speed is related to ______________________________

______________________________.

Quiz Yourself

1. How is motion defined? Give two examples where it can be seen.

2. Draw the trajectory of Spot to his food with a red line and the displacement with a blue arrow.

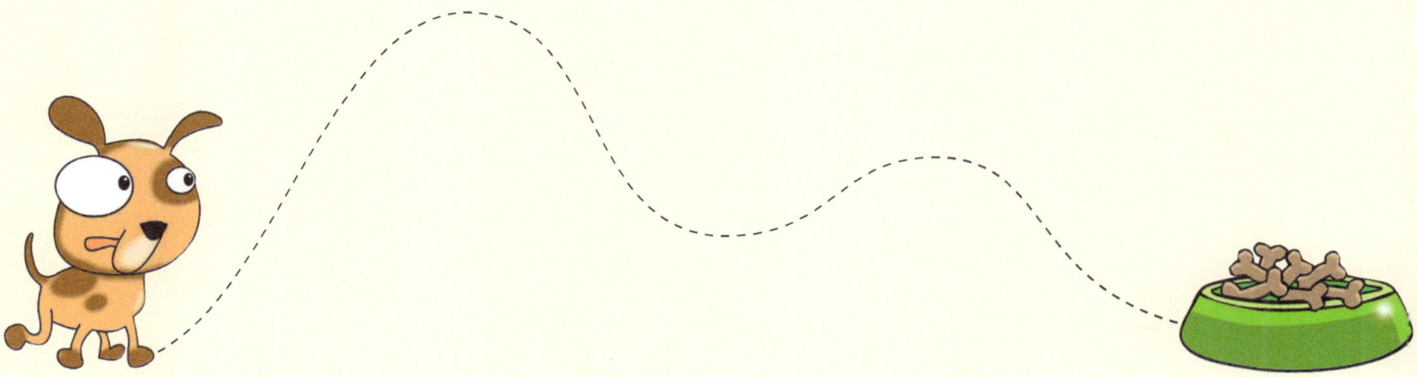

3. Look at the image.

a. How long does it take the cyclist to travel 15 kilometers?

b. Calculate her speed during the race.

Section 2
The Effects of Force

Connecting

Force

When you move a box or lift up your backpack, you are using **force**. But what is force? It is defined as the interaction between two or more objects that can:

– cause a change in the movements of the interacting objects.
– start an object moving or stop an object moving.
– change the shape of, or deform, an object.

One body or object applies the force, and one receives the force.

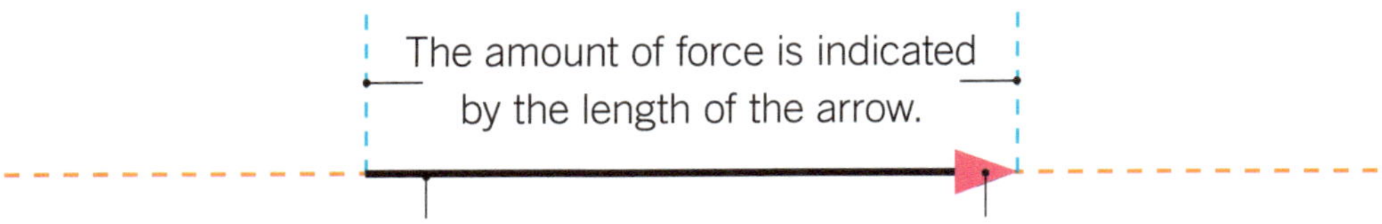

The arrow shows the **direction** in which the force acts. The direction can be vertical (up or down), horizontal (left or right) or diagonal (a combination of up or down with left or right).

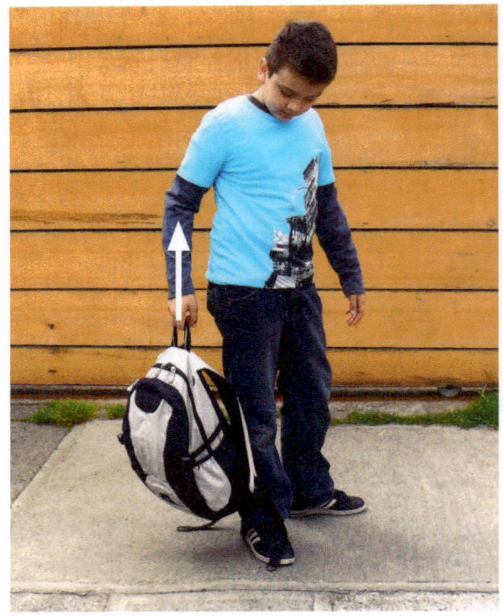

In the image, the boy is **exerting** force and the backpack is receiving force. The arrow represents the force the boy is exerting.

There are two types of force:

Contact Force
This type of force is physical. The body exerting the force is in physical contact with the receiving body. Example: someone pushing a box.

Noncontact Force
In this type of force, the body exerting the force is not in physical contact with the receiving body. Example: a magnet attracting paper clips.

Practicing

1. Look at the images. Mark the object exerting force in [blue] and the one receiving force in [red]. Identify

2. Collect a magnet and two paper clips. Put the clips on the table and move the magnet close to them.

a. What happened? Draw your observations. Observe

b. What type of force is seen in this case? Interpret

____

c. Separate the paper clips from the magnet. What type of force did you apply? Identify

____

Summarizing

Force is ____.

One body ____________________ force while the other ____________________ fcrce.

There are two general types of force: ______________________________.

Connecting

The Effects of Force on Objects

1. Collect a rubber band and a piece of clay. Experiment

a. What happened to the shape of the rubber band and clay when you applied force?

____

b. Which of the objects returns to its normal shape when force is no longer applied?

____

In the previous activity, you observed that when force is applied to a rubber band and to clay, they change shape. This shows that force can deform certain bodies. However, the two objects changed in different ways. Objects can be classified according to their reaction to force.

Rigid

Rigid objects only change when a very strong force is applied. Some examples of rigid bodies are iron and steel.

Elastic

Elastic objects return to their original shape when force is not being applied to them. Some examples of elastic bodies are rubber bands and metal springs.

Plastic

Plastic objects do not return to their original shape when force is not being applied. Some examples of plastic bodies are gum and clay.

Practicing

2. Collect the following materials: a scale, a metal spring, a 30 cm ruler and five objects with different masses. The objects could be: a pencil, an eraser, a pencil sharpener, a pencil case and a notebook.

a. Use the scale to measure the mass of the five objects. Use the ruler to measure the length of the metal spring (without stretching it). Measure

b. Hang the first object from the pencil, as shown in the image. Measure the length of the spring now. Do the same with the other four objects and record your results on the table. Record

Object	Mass (grams)	Length of the Metal Spring (centimeters)

c. Do the objects apply force to the spring? What type? Relate

____

d. Observe the spring when you apply force and when you stop. What kind of object is it? Interpret

____

e. Does the mass of each object influence the deformation of the spring? Explain. Explain

____

____

Summarizing

Forces can ______________ objects. According to an object's reaction to being deformed, it can be classified as: ______________, ______________ or ______________.

Connecting

The Effects of Force on Direction of Motion

Look at the following picture. Does the tennis ball always move in the same direction?

Remember that the direction of a force can be vertical (up or down), horizontal (left or right) or diagonal (a combination or up or down with left or right).

During a tennis match, the ball is constantly in motion. It changes direction each time the players apply force to the ball by hitting it with their rackets.

As in tennis, there are many other situations where **force can cause changes in the movement of a body** (object). An example is when you are sitting on a swing (suspended seat) and someone pushes you.

1. Find a marble (small glass ball) and place it on your desk. Push it lightly so that it moves.

a. What would happen if you applied an **opposing** force to its direction of motion? Describe

____

____

b. What would happen if you applied force in a different direction? Describe

____

____

A body in motion can change direction when a force is applied to it from the front, side or back. For example, if the body were headed diagonally and it was hit from the side, it might change its direction to straight, or if it were traveling straight and it was hit from the front, it would move in the opposite (negative) direction.

The Effects of Force on Speed of Motion

Force can change the shape of a body and also the direction of motion. But can it change its speed? Yes! In fact, every time a force is applied to a body, it can **change its speed**.

2. Use a toy car to analyze the following situations. Experiment

a. Place the car on the table and keep it steady. Then apply force.

If force is applied to a body **at rest**, it will start moving. Therefore, force changes the speed of the body.

not moving

b. Place the car on the table and apply only enough force to make it move it slowly. Then apply more force in the same direction as the motion.

If force is applied to a body in motion in the **same** direction, the body's speed will **increase**.

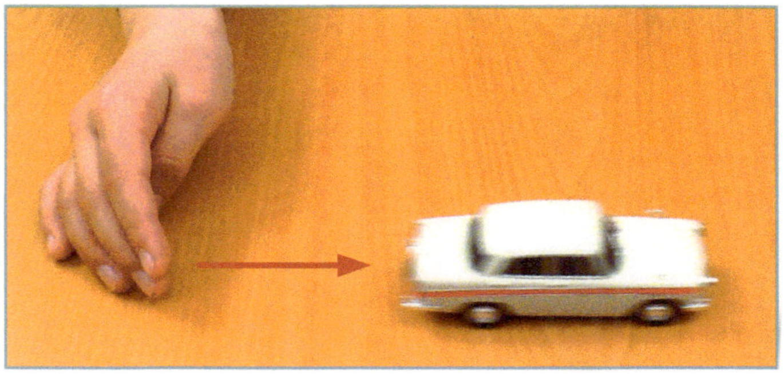

c. Make the car move slowly again. Then apply force that opposes the motion.

If an **opposing** force is applied to a body in motion, the body's speed will **decrease** or the direction of the motion will change.

Education through Values

Throughout the world, seat belts are considered the most important security measure in cars. It is important to always use one when you are in a car so you do not get hurt if the car stops suddenly. Also, this is a good way to respect traffic laws.

Practicing

3. Use arrows to represent the force needed to produce each change. Represent

Move a toy that is at rest.

Change the direction of motion of a marble.

Decrease the speed of a toy train.

Increase the speed of a shopping cart.

Summarizing

Force — can change → [ ] / [ ]

Quiz Yourself

1. Place a ping-pong ball on the table and push it with your finger.

   a. Why does the ball move? Explain.

   ____

   ____

   ____

   ____

   ____

   ____

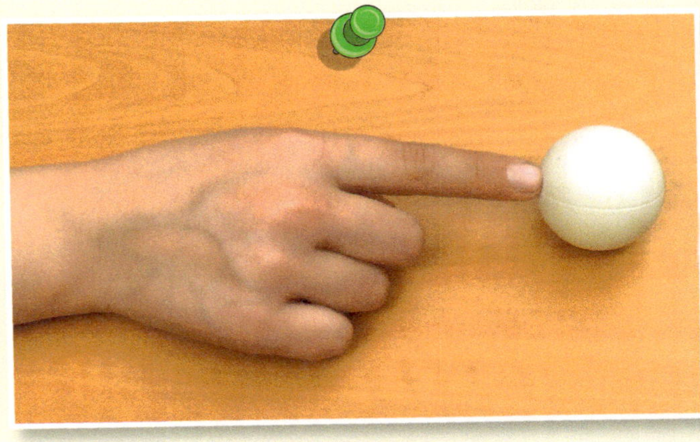

   b. What type of force did you apply?

   ____

   c. What is exerting force?

   ____

   d. What is receiving force?

   ____

   • Push the ball again.

   e. Apply force in the same direction as its motion. What happens? Explain.

   ____

   ____

   f. Apply force in the opposite direction to its motion. What happens? Explain.

   ____

   ____

   g. Could force change the shape of the ball? Explain.

   ____

   ____

Building a Spring Scale

Basic Framework

In order to measure force, an instrument called a **spring scale** is used. It is made from a metal spring and a measuring scale that shows the amount of force being applied to the spring.

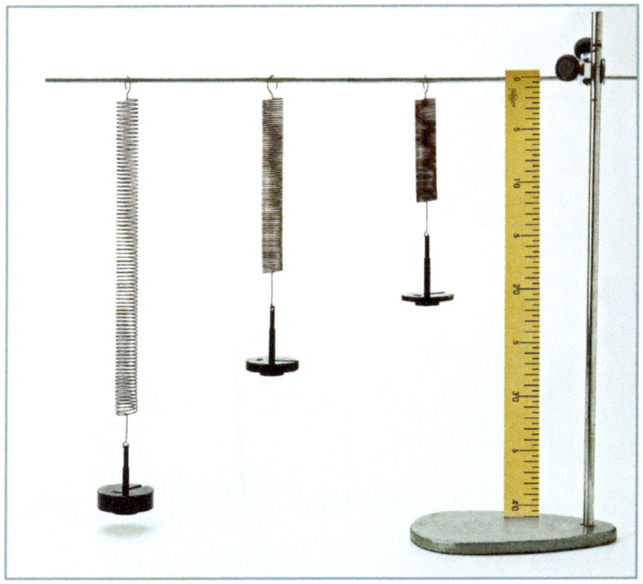

Observation

Observe the image.

Why are the springs different lengths?

___

___

___

Research Question

What is the function of the metal spring in a spring scale?

Hypothesis

A spring scale uses the deformation of a spring to measure force.

Prediction

Mark the prediction you think is correct.

- ☐ The deformation of the spring in the spring scale increases when **more** force is applied.
- ☐ The deformation of the spring in the spring scale increases when **less** force is applied.

Experimental Procedure

1. Collect the following supplies: a metal spring, a set of 10 weights from 50–500 grams, a piece of wood that is 30 centimeters long and 5 centimeters wide, a nail, a hammer, a paper clip and **Activity Card 8**.
2. Glue the graph paper from the activity card on the piece of wood.
3. Hammer the nail into one end of the wood.
4. Attach the spring to the nail.

5. On the other end of the spring, connect the paper clip. Bend the paper clip so it has a hook at the bottom.
6. Mark the length of the spring on the graph paper and label it **0**.
7. Hang a 50 gram weight on the end of the paper clip, and mark the length of the spring. Label this point according to the table on **Activity Card 8**, which shows the amount of force applied by each of the weights.
8. Remove the 50 gram weight and hang the 100 gram weight. Mark the new length of the spring and label the applied force.
9. Follow the same steps with the 150, 200, 250, 300, 350, 400, 450 and 500 gram weights.
10. You just built a spring scale that allows you to measure force from 0 to 5 Newtons.

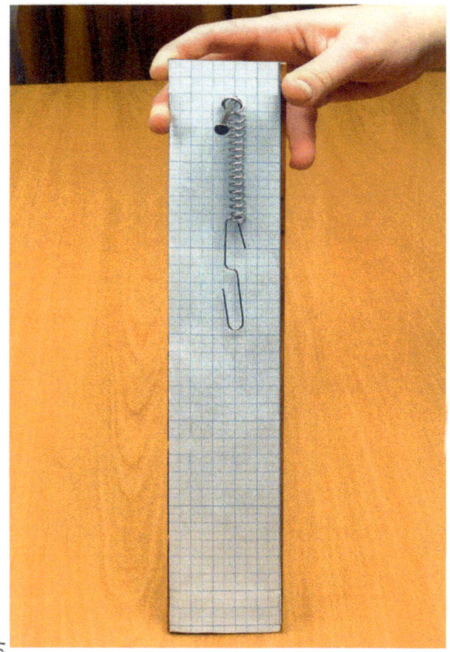

Results

1. What happened to the spring as the weight increased?

____

____

Interpreting and Analyzing Results

1. What determines the length of the spring?

____

____

2. Was your prediction the same as your results?

____

____

To compare and contrast means to find similarities and differences. In this case, we looked at similarities and differences between your predictions and the actual results. This comparison allows you to test or prove your research question.

Conclusion

1. What is the function of the spring in the spring scale?

____

____

Let's Check!

1. Match each concept with its description.

points
/ 4

Motion	The path a body travels along when in motion.
Displacement	Relates distance traveled and time taken.
Trajectory	The arrow that connects the initial position to the final position.
Speed	The change in the position of a body.

2. Martin wants to go to the ice cream shop. Represent his possible trajectory with a red line and his displacement with a green arrow.

points
/ 2

3. Amelie's dog likes to run on the beach. If it takes the dog 5 seconds to run 10 meters, what is its speed?

points
/ 2

4. What is the effect of applying force in each case?

points
/ 3

____________________ ____________________ ____________________

____________________ ____________________ ____________________

5. Look at the image and respond.

points
/ 4

a. Why does the toy car move? Explain.

____

b. What object is exerting force? What object is receiving force?

____

c. What is the effect of force on the car?

____

Different Forces

Connecting

Frictional Force

1. Collect an eraser, tape, a piece of carpet and a piece of paper.
Experiment

Tape the piece of carpet onto the table. Place the eraser on top and push it with your hand.	Tape the piece of paper to the table. Place the eraser on top and push it with your hand.
	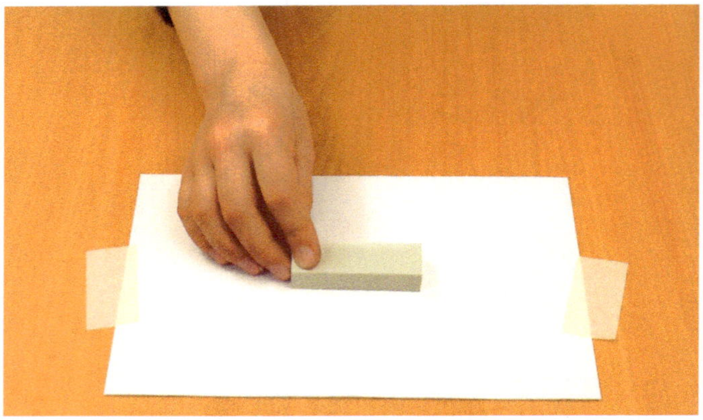

a. In which situation is it more difficult to move the eraser? Why do you think that is?

____

____

____

When pushing the eraser over both surfaces, you can feel that it is easier to move the eraser on paper than on carpet.

When two bodies are in contact, in this case the eraser and the surface (carpet or paper), the **interaction** between the two is called **friction** or **frictional force**. The strength of this interaction depends on the characteristics of the surfaces that are touching. Some surfaces are **porous**, like the carpet, and others are smooth, like the paper. The force of friction **opposes the motion of objects**.

In the experiment you just completed, the frictional force was stronger when you pushed the eraser on the carpet because it is more porous than the paper.

Challenge

Find a marble and a tilted surface. What kind of surface makes the ball roll the slowest? Which surface lets it roll the fastest? Do not forget to record your results.

2. Place a cardboard box on the floor and push it. Then put a few books inside the box and push it again. Experiment

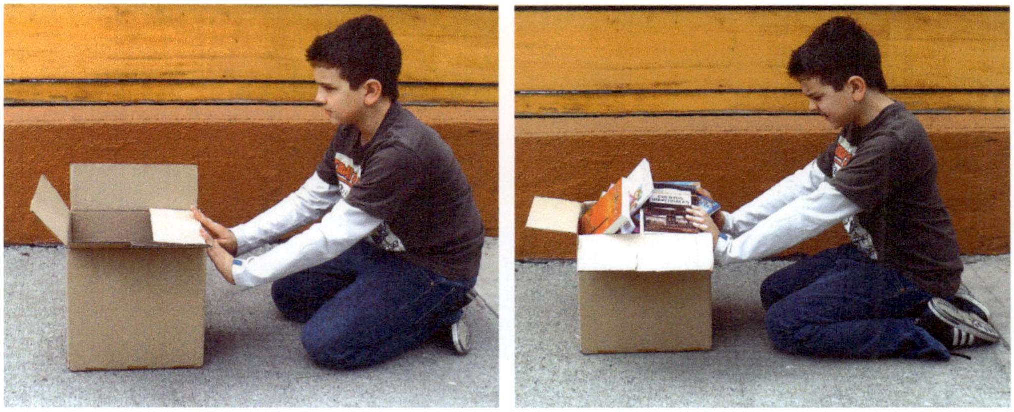

a. In which case is it more difficult to move the box? Explain.

____

____

If you push an empty box across the floor, it moves easily. But if you fill it with objects, like notebooks or books, you will have to push harder, or exert more force. When the weight of the box increases, it exerts more force on the floor. This increases the force of friction between the surfaces.

Therefore, frictional force depends on different factors, such as the characteristics of the bodies that are in contact and their mass.

Staying Healthy

Many surfaces have very little friction, such as ceramic floors or floors when they are wet. When you walk on surfaces like these, always be extra careful so you do not slip and fall.

slip: slide unintentionally

Practicing

3. In which case is the force of friction between the two surfaces greater? Apply

☐ When an empty pencil case is pushed on a table.

☐ When a full pencil case is pushed on a table.

Summarizing

Friction opposes the ______________________________ of objects. It depends on ____.

Connecting

Gravitational Force

gently

1. Hold an object in your hand. Softly toss it into the air. What happens? Describe

Look at these photographs.

As you can see, the cube reaches a certain height and then falls back into the person's hand. This is because our planet has a force that attracts objects to its surface. It is called the **force of gravity** or **gravitational force**. It is a noncontact or distance force.

The amount of gravity that earth exerts on a body depends on the body's mass. For example, if we compare the gravitational force that earth exerts on a car with the gravitational force it exerts on an ant, the force of gravity on the car is stronger. This is because the car has a greater mass than the ant. The **weight** of an object is the force exerted on it by gravity.

Sometimes we use the words **weight** and **mass** as synonyms. However, the concepts are different. Mass is the amount of matter in a body. Weight is the measurement of how strongly the force of gravity is pulling on a body.

Fun Fact!

The force of gravity is not only felt on earth. Its effects can be felt on other planets and celestial bodies, like the moon. There is also a force that attracts the moon to earth, and one that attracts the planets in the solar system to the sun. The force keeps them constantly in orbit.

Practicing

2. On which body does gravity exert the most force? Mark with a ✓. Identify

☐ 

☐ 

☐ 

3. Look at the photographs and answer. Why is the force that is exerted in both photos the same? Apply

____

____

____

Summarizing

The force of gravity is ____.

Connecting

Magnetic Force

1. Collect a magnet and a few paper clips. Move the magnet toward the clips. What happens? Describe

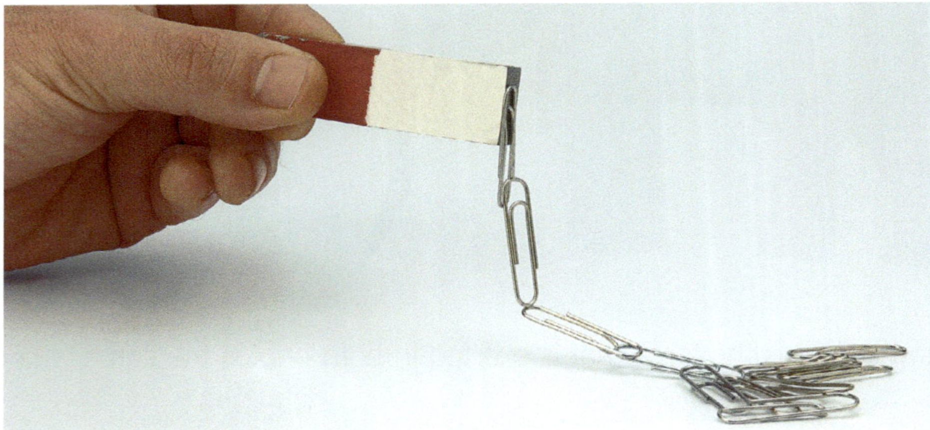

Each magnet has two sides or **poles** with opposing characteristics. One is north (positive) and one is south (negative).

The force that attracts the paper clips to the magnet is called **magnetic force**. It is a noncontact force.

Magnetic force can **attract** or **repel**. In the case of the paper clips and the magnet, the force at work is attraction.

2. Find two magnets with the poles marked north and south. Complete the following activities. Experiment

Challenge

Why are the ends of earth called the North and South Poles? How does a compass work? Draw a picture to answer these questions.

a. Move the north side of one magnet toward the north side of the other. What happens?

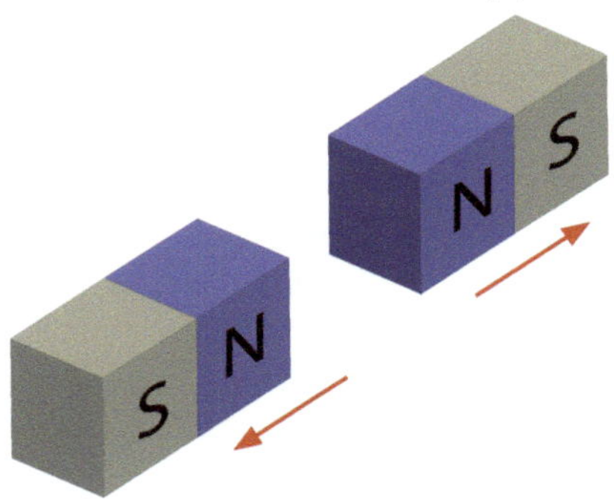

The magnetic force in this case is **repulsion** because the magnets do not come together.

b. Next, move the north pole of one magnet toward the south pole of the other. What happens?

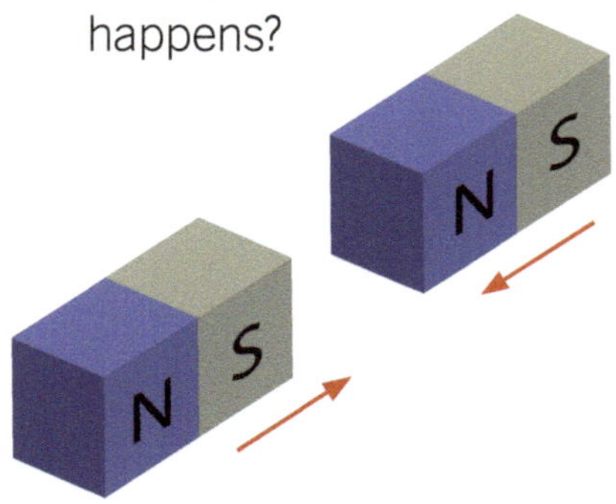

In this case, the magnetic force is **attraction** because the magnets come together.

c. Finally, move the south pole of one magnet toward the south pole of the other. What happens?

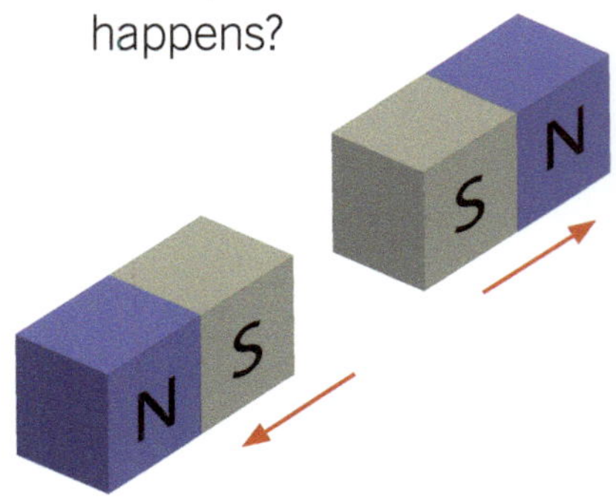

The magnetic force in this case is **repulsion** because the magnets do not come together.

Electric Force

Have you ever taken off a wool (sheep hair) sweater and noticed it made your hair stand up? Or have you felt a little **shock** when you touched another person? These situations are caused by **electric force**. Electric force corresponds to the interaction between bodies that have an **electric charge**.

Is there interaction between bodies with electric charges? Just like magnetic force, electric force can also establish connections between bodies.

When charged bodies are moved toward each other, their interaction depends on the electric charge of each one. Some interactions are:

Two bodies with a negative electric charge repel each other, so the electrical force between them is **repulsion**.

Two bodies with a positive electric charge repel each other, so the electrical force between them is **repulsion**.

One body with a negative electric charge and another with a positive electric charge attract each other, so the electrical force between them is **attraction**.

Word Focus

An **electric charge** is a characteristic that some bodies develop through interactions such as rubbing (moving against with pressure) against another body. Objects that have an electric charge interact with each other. There are positive and negative charges.

A positive charge is represented with a + symbol and a negative charge with a – symbol.

Did You Know...?

Static electricity is what makes your hair stand on end after you go down a slide or rub a balloon on your head. It happens when the electric charge on the surface of one object is transferred to another object that has less charge.

Fun Fact!

When a body has no electric charge, it is called neutral. Neutral means that it has equal numbers of positive and negative particles.

Practicing

3. Go to **Cutout 8** on **page 169**.

a. Write N for the north pole and S for the south pole on each magnet. Identify

b. Glue the magnets according to the interaction indicated. Apply

Repulsion	Attraction

4. Maryanne rubbed two balloons on her hair and then put them together. Think of the different electrical interactions. What do you think happened to the balloons? Infer

____

____

Summarizing

Magnetic force is ____.

Electric force is ____.

Quiz Yourself

1. Look at the images and respond.

a. In which case would the box be easier to move?

____

b. What force opposes the box's motion?

____

2. Look at the images and respond.

a. In which case does the girl need to apply more force to carry her backpack? Explain.

____

b. In which case is the gravitational force on the backpack stronger? Explain.

____

What Did You Learn?

1. Jack put an ant on a piece of notebook paper. While the ant moved, he timed it with a stopwatch and his friend, Andrew, traced the ant's movement with a pencil. After five seconds, the drawing looked like this:

points
/ 3

a. Mark the ant's trajectory in blue and its displacement in green.

b. If the ant moved a distance of 20 cm in 5 seconds, at what speed did it move?

2. Every day Pauly counts his steps on the way to school. Which of the following is he calculating by counting his steps? Mark the correct answer with a ✔.

point
/ 1

A. Distance traveled.

B. Displacement.

C. Speed.

D. Time.

3. What are the effects of the following types of force? Explain using examples.

points
/ 3

Frictional Force	Gravitational Force	Magnetic Force

Final Evaluation

4. Go to **Cutout 9** on **page 169**. Glue the images that show the following effects when force is applied.

points /3

Change in Shape	Change in Direction	Change in Speed

Scientific Skill: Compare and contrast

5. Answer.

points /6

a. What would happen to a piece of wood and a rubber ball if force were applied to each? Make a prediction.

____

____

b. Collect a piece of wood and a rubber ball. Push on each object with your hands. What happens? Write down your observations.

____

____

c. Were your predictions the same as your observations?

____

____

Find Test 4 Study Page

Unit 5

The Earth Moves

Key Words

external
internal
promote
produce
layer

In this unit you will learn to:

- describe the different characteristics of the earth's layers.
- explain changes of the earth's surface.
- use diagrams to communicate ideas, explanations and observations.

What Do You Know?

Initial Evaluation

1. Look at the picture and mark with a ✔ the village that will be more affected by a tsunami.
2. Mark the village that will be more affected by a volcanic eruption with an ✖.

Scientific Skill: Communicate

3. In Chile, on February 2010, at 3:34 a.m., there was an earthquake with a magnitude of 8.8 on the Richter scale. The epicenter was 43 kilometers southwest of Cobquecura, in the Biobio region. Use this information to answer the questions below.
   a. What facts do you think are the most important? Which facts would you share with the community?

   ____

   ____

   b. Make a poster to share this information with your community.

Section 1
The Structure of the Earth

Connecting

The Components of Our Planet

Imagine that you are lying on the beach. In this moment, you are in contact with the **atmosphere**, the **geosphere** and the **hydrosphere**. Have you ever heard these names? They are the three principal components of the earth.

The Atmosphere
The atmosphere is the mass of gases surrounding our planet. It is about 500 km thick and consists of a mixture of several gases. This includes oxygen, a gas necessary for life for the majority of living things on earth.

The Hydrosphere
The hydrosphere is all the water on our planet. This includes oceans, rivers, lakes, lagoons, underground water, polar ice, glaciers and the water found as vapor in the atmosphere. Water is our most abundant resource, and it covers most of the earth's surface.

The Geosphere
The geosphere is the solid part of earth. It consists of the continents, islands, mountains and all the land at the bottom of rivers, lakes and oceans. The geosphere includes the interior of our planet, too.

Fun Fact!

Today it is known that the earth has a round (spherical) shape, also called a geoid, but there was a time when people thought the earth was flat.

Practicing

1. Go to **Cutout 10** on **page 169**. Glue each of the earth's components in the correct place and write down its characteristics. Describe

Atmosphere	Hydrosphere	Geosphere

Summarizing

Earth	consists of the	

Connecting

The Geosphere

Imagine that we are drilling through the ground with a large drill for a long time. How deep could we go? What could we find? If we could do this, we would see the layers of the geosphere.

The geosphere consists of three layers: the **crust**, the **mantle** and the **core**.

a tool used for making holes

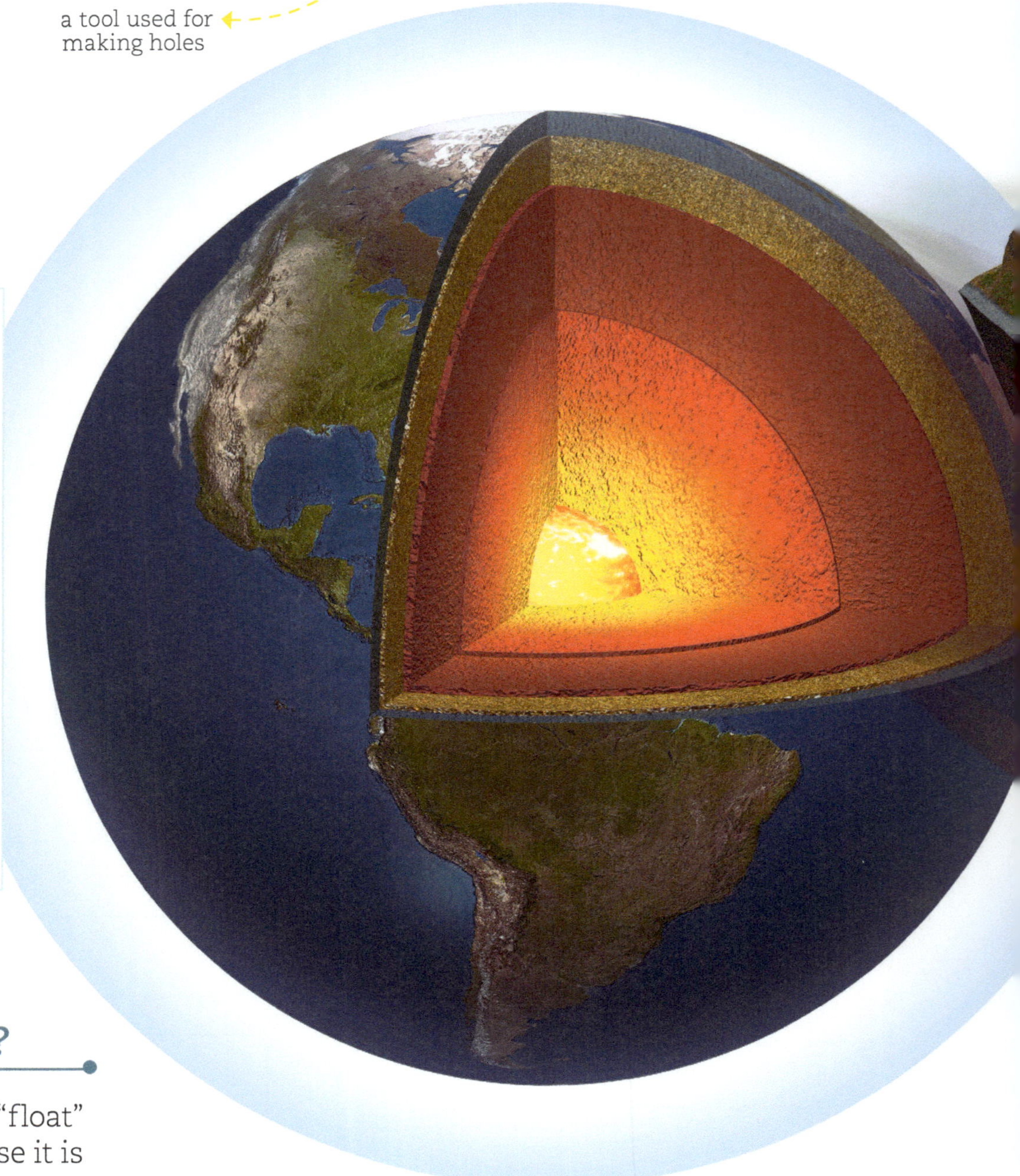

The Crust
This is the cold, outer layer of the earth. The continents, mountains and ocean floor are all part of this layer. It consists of solid materials like rocks. There are some areas where this layer is very thin, like the ocean floor, where it can be only 7 kilometers thick, and others where it is thicker, like in the mountains, where it can be more than 60 kilometers thick.

Did You Know...?

The crust is said to "float" on the mantle because it is less dense.

The Mantle
This layer can be almost 2,900 kilometers thick in places and principally consists of solid rock. The mantle varies in temperature from 100 °C near the crust to 3,000 °C near the core.
At about 600 kilometers deep, the mantle has a liquid layer called the asthenosphere.

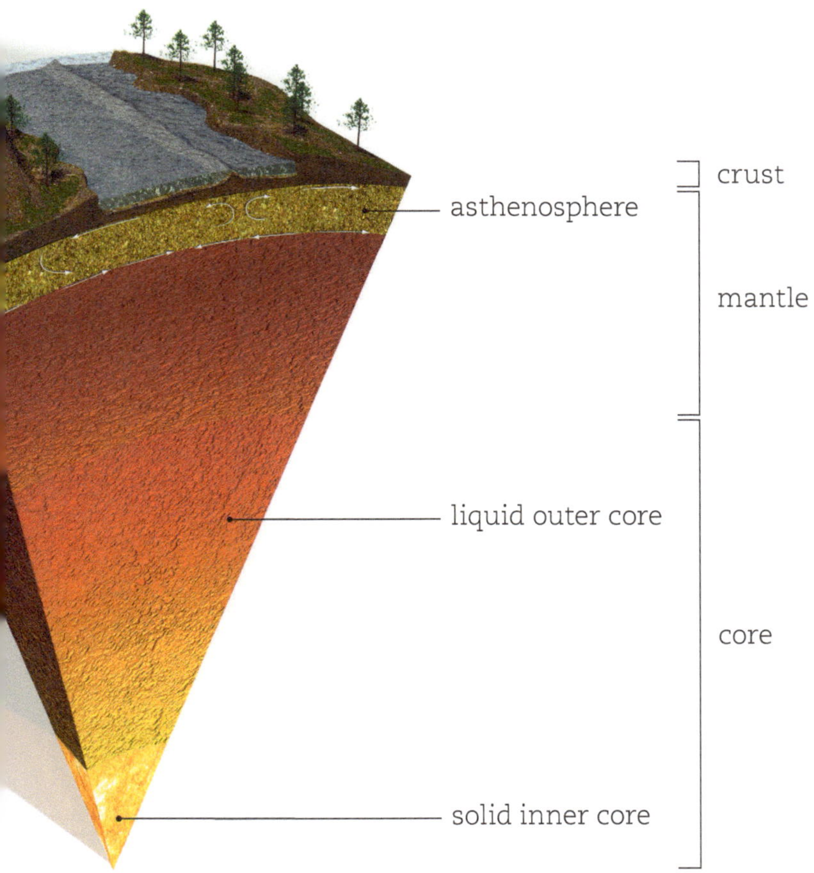

a silvery-white metal

The Core
This is the deepest layer of the earth and is nearly 3,500 kilometers thick.
It is composed of iron and nickel, and its temperature reaches 6,000 °C. The core is divided into two parts: the liquid **outer core** and the solid **inner core**.

Remember!

° is read as "degrees," and "C" is read as Celsius.

The farther we travel toward the center of the earth, the higher the temperature is.

Did You Know...?

The inner core is 70 percent of the size of the moon.

Practicing

1. Complete the diagram with the names of the layers of the geosphere. Identify

2. Complete the following comparison chart of the characteristics of the layers of the geosphere.

Layer	Composition	Thickness	Temperature
Crust			
Mantle			
Core			

Summarizing

The geosphere consists of the

Quiz Yourself

Ask an adult to cut the Styrofoam ball in half.

1. Make a miniature geosphere using a Styrofoam ball cut in half. Use tempera paint and colored pencils to color it like the earth.

Paint the outside of each half of the ball. Paint the oceans blue and the continents green or brown.

On the inside of each half, draw the layers of the geosphere. Use a different color for each.

a. Write the name of each layer on the model.

b. Describe the characteristics of each layer of the geosphere.

Layer	Characteristics
Crust	
Mantle	
Core	

Section

2 The Earth Changes

Connecting

The Lithosphere and Tectonic Plates

What would you think if someone said to you that the surface of the earth is like a jigsaw puzzle? The most external zone of the earth is called the **lithosphere**. It consists of the oceanic crust, the continental crust and the outer part of the mantle.

The lithosphere is not one solid mass, but instead is composed of different pieces that fit together, similar to a puzzle. These pieces are called **tectonic plates**.

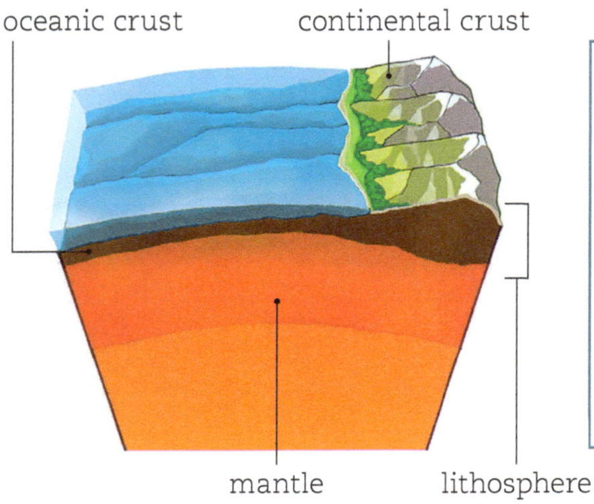

tectonic plates

Fun Fact!

One modern theory is that in the past the continents were all connected together as one giant continent called Pangaea. It separated because of the movements of the tectonic plates.

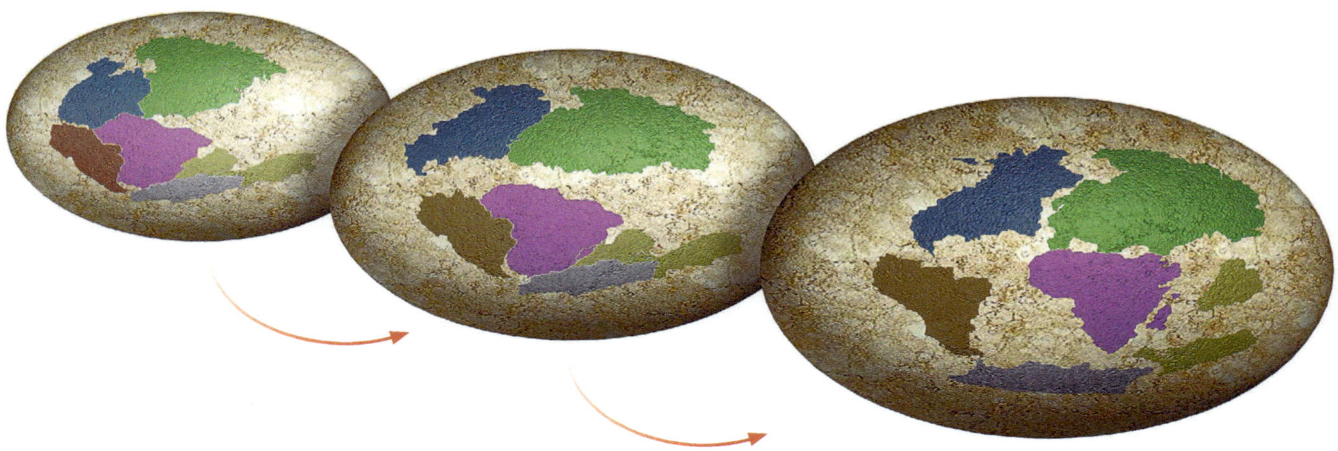

The Movement of Tectonic Plates

Tectonic plates are never at a **standstill**—that is, they are in constant motion. As they are located above the more fluid mantle zone, they can move. When tectonic plates move, three interactions can take place:

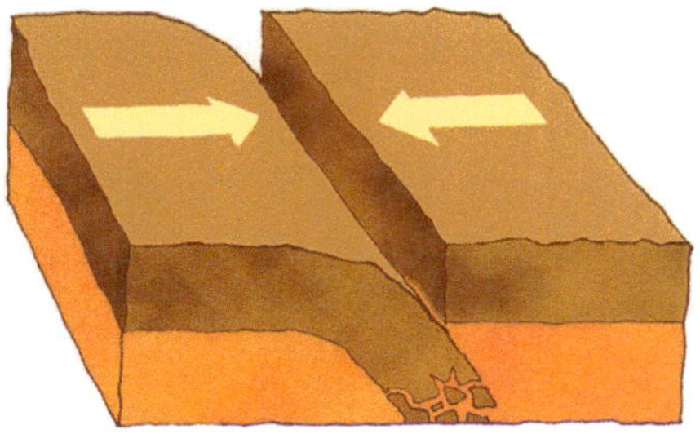

The tectonic plates move closer together, and one goes under the other.

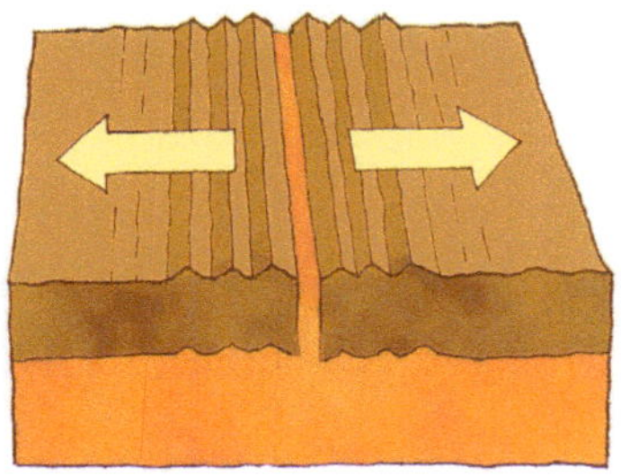

The tectonic plates move away from each other.

The tectonic plates rub together.

The different tectonic movements are responsible for the great changes that the earth has experienced and continues to experience. Some changes take place slowly, such as the **formation of mountains** and **volcanoes**, and others take place very quickly, like **earthquakes**.

Practicing

1. Go to **Activity Card 9**. Cut out the tectonic plates along the red lines. Put the puzzle together. Then answer.

a. Which tectonic plates are in contact? Give examples. Identify

____

____

b. Which cities are located above tectonic plate contact zones? Name three. Associate

____

Summarizing

The lithosphere is the ____________________ part of the earth. It is composed of ____________________

____

and it is divided into ________________________________.

Connecting

Earthquakes

The tectonic plates of the lithosphere are constantly moving, even though we do not notice. However, sometimes large movements of the plates cause movement on the earth's surface, called **tremors** and earthquakes.

In certain areas, these movements have great destructive power. The point of origin of these movements is called a **hypocenter**.

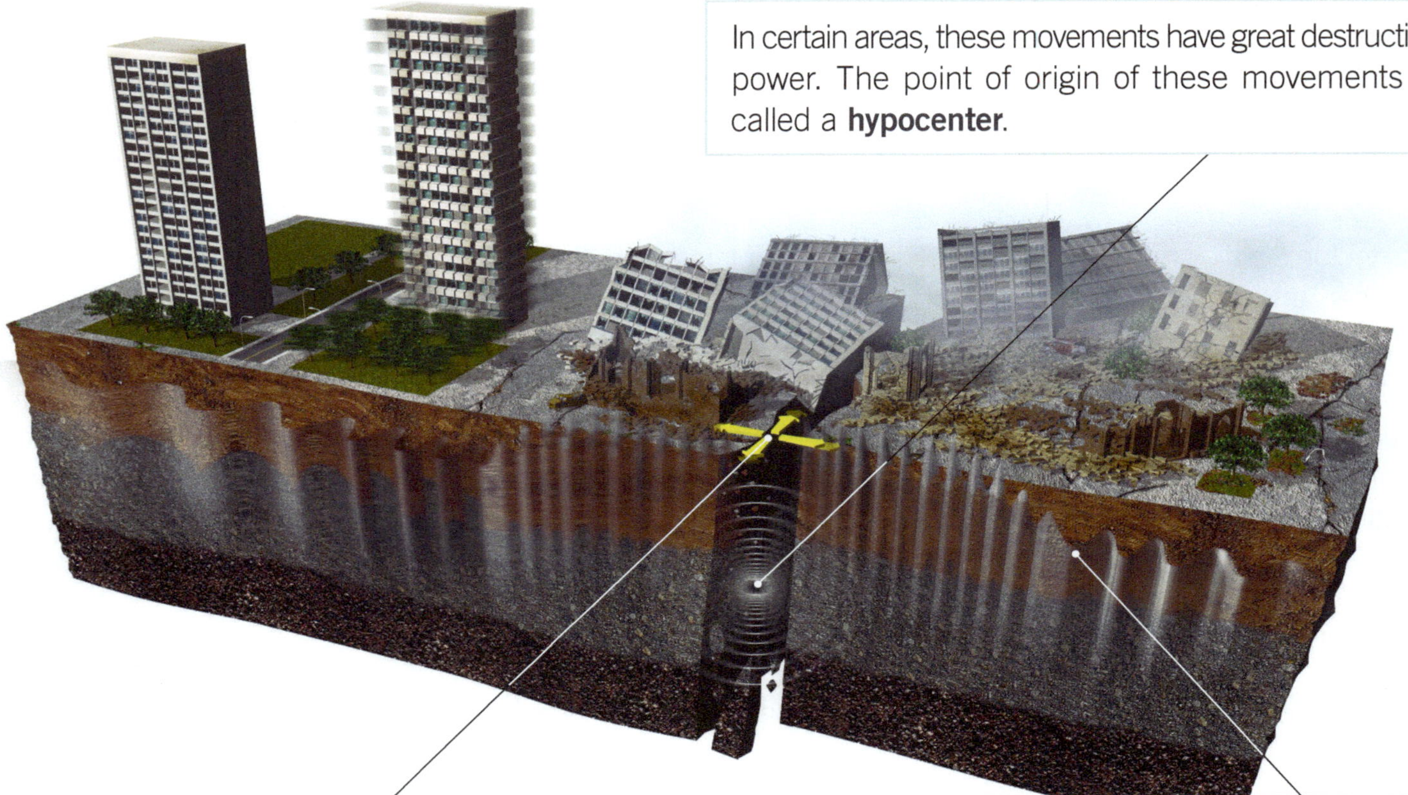

The point on the surface exactly above the hypocenter is called the **epicenter**. It is here where the tremor or earthquake is felt with the greatest intensity.

The movement that originates in the hypocenter quickly travels through the lithosphere in all directions.

Earthquakes are measured using two scales: Richter and Mercalli. The **Richter scale** measures the energy released in an earthquake, whereas the **Mercalli scale** measures the damage caused.

Fun Fact!

Scientifically speaking, there is no definition for the concept of an earthquake. However, the term is used to refer to a tremor that causes observable damage to buildings and other structures.

Major Recent Earthquakes

Most major earthquakes take place in a zone of volcanic activity surrounding the Pacific Ocean known as the Ring of Fire, which passes through Japan, Chile, Alaska, Mexico and Indonesia, among other countries. Some major recent earthquakes include:

Chile (1960)
The intensity of this earthquake was 9.6 on the Richter scale. The city of Valdivia sank almost four meters. It is the strongest earthquake ever recorded.

sank → moved down

Sumatra (2004)
This undersea earthquake, measuring 9.1–9.3 on the Richter scale, caused a massive tsunami that killed over 230,000 people.

Chile (2010)
This earthquake measured 8.8 on the Richter scale and lasted for over three minutes. Around 500 people were killed.

lasted → continued

Japan (2011)
This 9.0 earthquake lasted around six minutes. It caused a tsunami that damaged nuclear power stations, resulting in the evacuation of over 200,000 people.

Practicing

1. Match each concept with its description.

Epicenter ●	● Movement of the earth's surface originating in the lithosphere.
Hypocenter ●	● Exact point where the seismic movement originates in the lithosphere.
Earthquake ●	● Point on the surface located directly above the hypocenter.

Summarizing

Earthquakes are movements on the earth's surface caused by ______________________________

______________________________. The Ring of Fire around the Pacific Ocean is the most **seismic** or **earthquake-prone** area in the world.

Connecting

Tsunamis

As you studied previously, movements in the lithosphere cause tremors or earthquakes that may result in serious damage on the earth's surface. In some cases, the epicenter is located at the bottom of the ocean, and both the oceanic crust and the water move. Such movements can create giant waves known as tsunamis, which can cause major disasters when they hit nearby coastal areas.

When the epicenter is located at the bottom of the ocean, both water and land move.

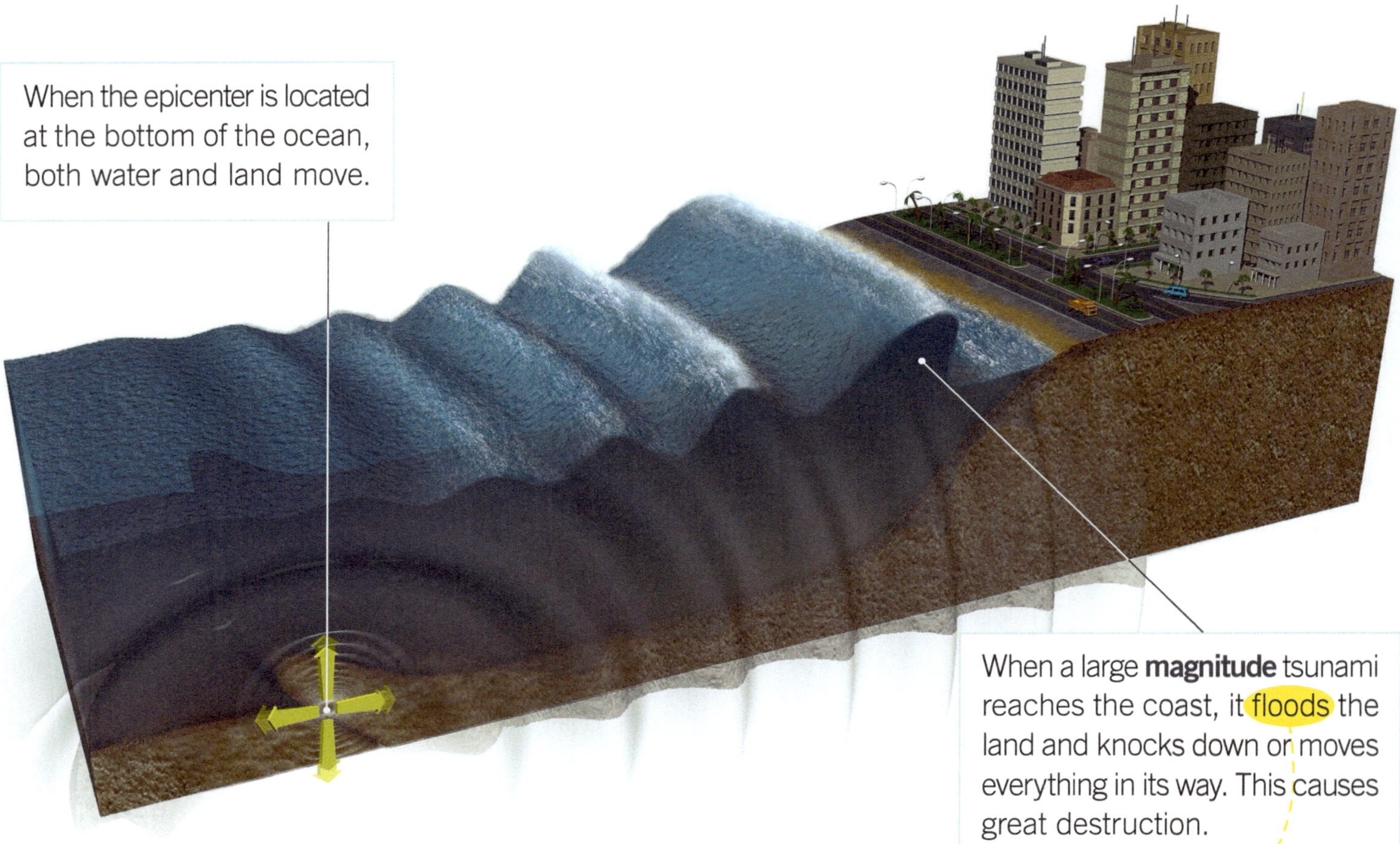

When a large **magnitude** tsunami reaches the coast, it floods the land and knocks down or moves everything in its way. This causes great destruction.

inundates

Did You Know...?

The 2004 earthquake in Sumatra created a massive tsunami that swept the coastal areas around the Indian Ocean. The tsunami reached over 20 meters high in some areas.

Fun Fact!

When earthquakes occur in places where the ocean is more than 6,000 meters deep, the waves can travel as fast as a commercial airplane (800 km/h).

Volcanoes

There is a third natural phenomenon related to the activity of the lithosphere: volcanism. A volcano is an opening in the earth's surface where materials can come out of the interior, like magma, ash, rocks and gases.

Fun Fact!

Magma is molten rock located inside the earth. (made liquid by heat)

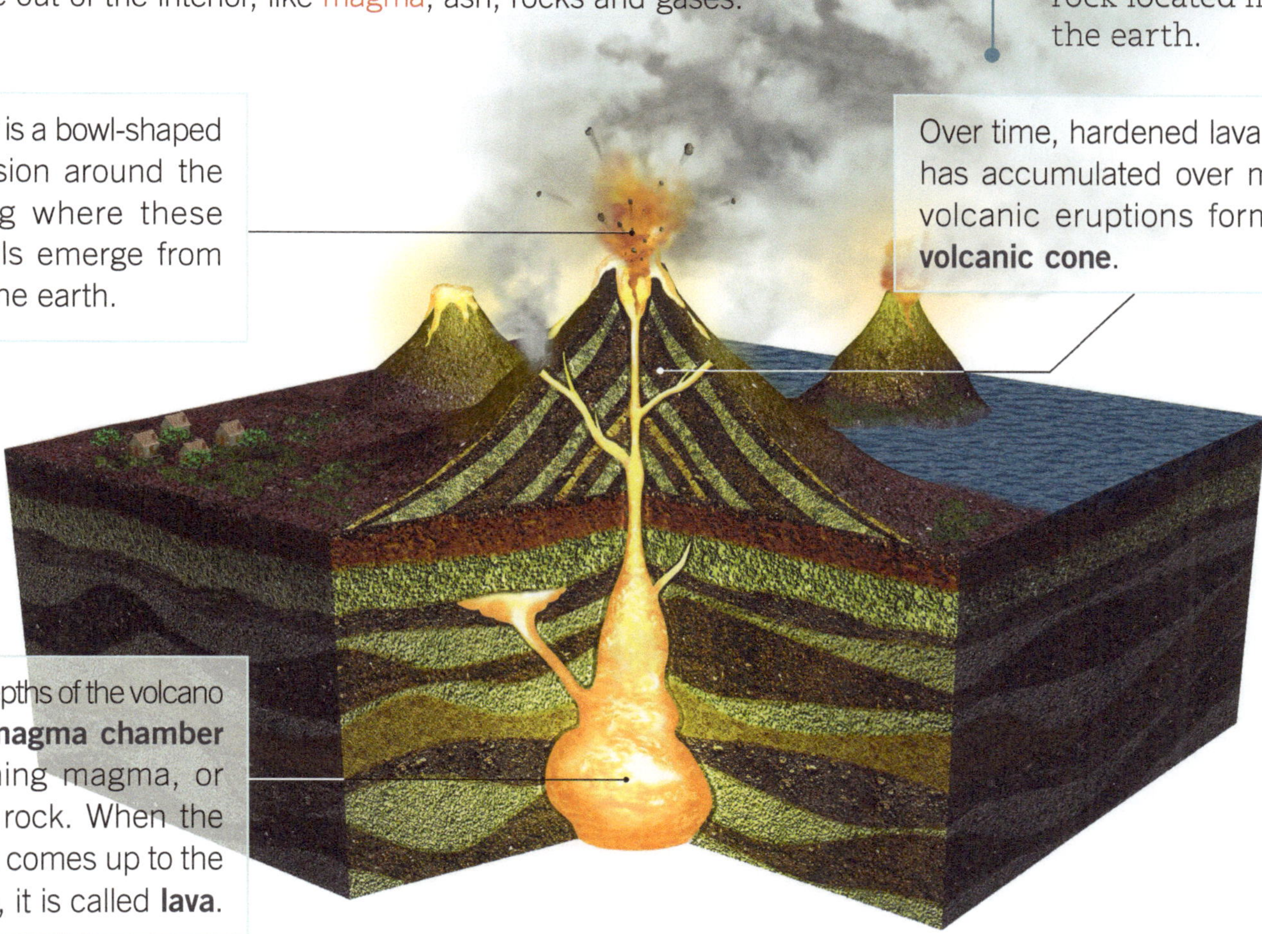

A **crater** is a bowl-shaped depression around the opening where these materials emerge from inside the earth.

Over time, hardened lava that has accumulated over many volcanic eruptions forms a **volcanic cone**.

In the depths of the volcano is the **magma chamber** containing magma, or molten rock. When the magma comes up to the surface, it is called **lava**.

Volcanic activity is diverse. Some volcanoes expel materials gently and continuously for years, and others have violent and sudden eruptions that cause damage and major changes to the earth's surface.

Did You Know...?

The most active volcano in the world is Kilauea on Hawaii. It has been erupting since 1952.

Practicing

1. What produces an earthquake? Explain

---

2. What is the difference between an epicenter and a hypocenter? Compare

---

---

3. What produces a tsunami? Explain

---

4. Write the names of the structures. Identify

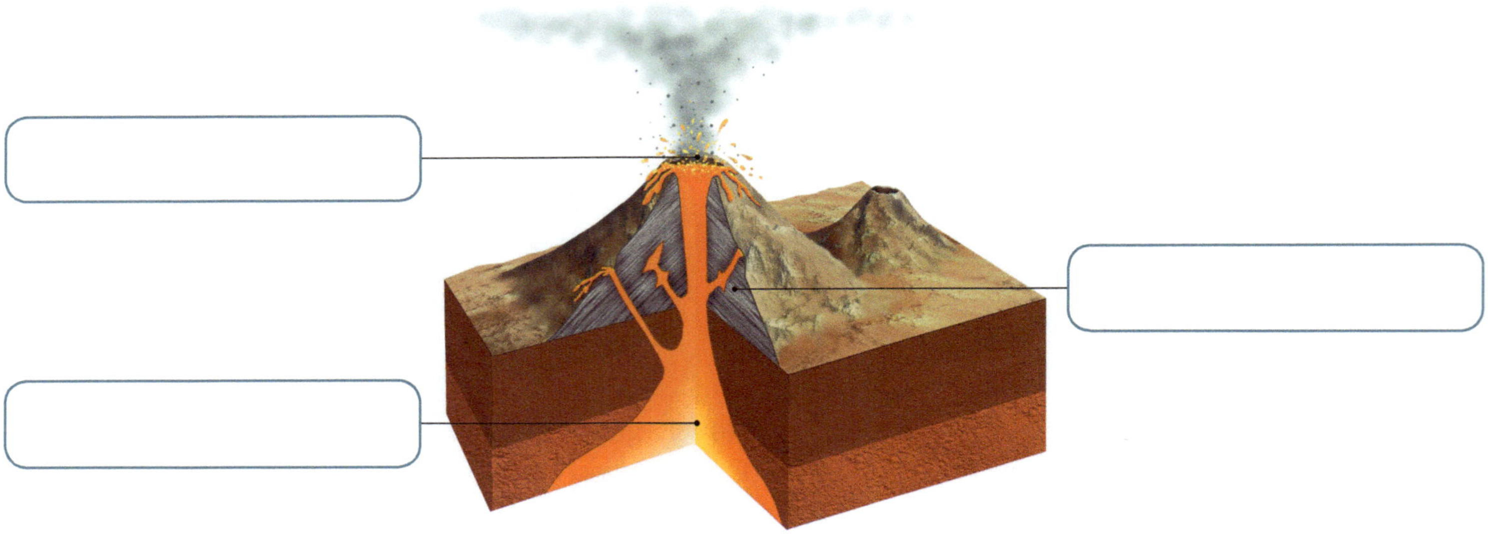

Summarizing

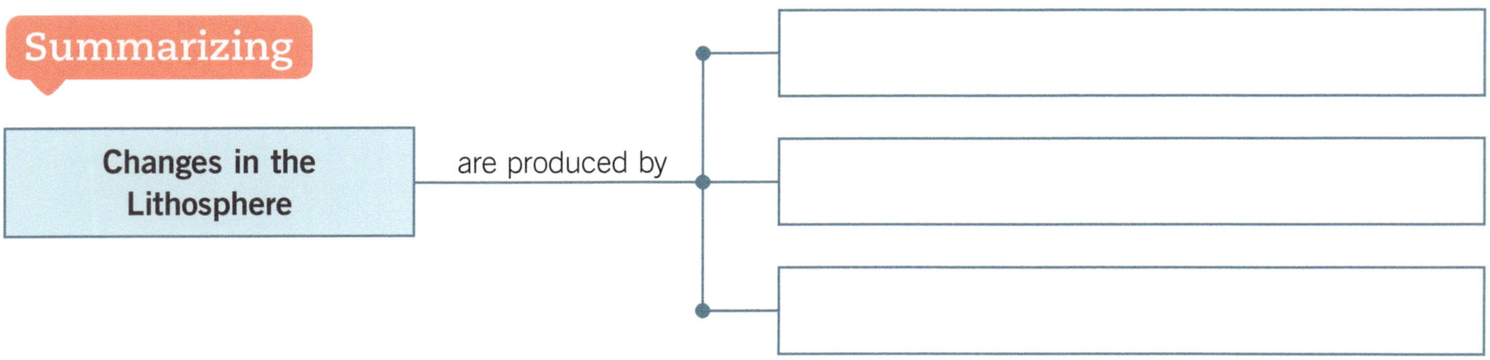

Quiz Yourself

1. Identify the phenomenon represented in each image and explain how it is produced.

2. What do earthquakes, tsunamis and volcanic eruptions have in common? Explain.

What Are the Effects of a Volcanic Eruption?

Basic Framework

Volcanic eruptions can cause serious damage because of the large amount of lava they expel. Many cities are located at the foot of a volcano, and therefore can be exposed to the damage caused by an eruption.

Observation

Look at the following picture.

If a volcanic eruption occurred, what changes could take place in the city near this volcano?

___

___

___

___

Research Question

What effects does a volcanic eruption have on nearby cities?

Hypothesis

The volcano expels volcanic materials that reach the city, causing damage.

Prediction

If you make a model of a city at the foot of a volcano, what would you observe when the volcano erupts?

___

___

Experimental Procedure

1. Form groups of three, and then find these materials: a 20 x 20 cm piece of cardboard, clay, a plastic cup, baking soda and white vinegar.

2. Place the cardboard around the cup, and use the clay to build a volcano, as shown in the picture.

3. Then build the city at the foot of the volcano.

4. Put two tablespoons of baking soda in the cup.
5. Carefully add a quarter cup of vinegar to the baking soda and observe what happens.

Results

1. How did the materials move out of the model volcano?

____

Interpreting and Analyzing Results

1. What does the overflowing of the baking soda and vinegar mixture from the volcano model represent?

____

Conclusion

1. Make a diagram explaining how the city was affected by the volcanic eruption.

When **communicating**, you are transmitting verbal or written information. This information can be shown through tables, diagrams, drawings and even through explanatory text.

What Did You Learn?

points
12

1. Draw a model showing the layers of the geosphere.

a. Label the picture with the name of each layer.

b. Write the characteristics of each layer. Think about thickness, composition and temperature.

____

____

____

____

____

2. Mark the correct answer with a ✔. As you travel toward the earth's core, the temperature:

point
1

A. Increases, and then decreases.

B. Does not change.

C. Decreases.

D. Increases.

Final Evaluation

3. What changes cause these phenomena to occur? Explain.

points ___ / 3

Earthquakes	
Tsunamis	
Volcanic Eruptions	

4. Complete the following chart with three actions we should do and three we should not do in a natural disaster emergency.

points ___ / 6

In a natural disaster emergency, we:	
should	should not

Scientific Skill: Communicate

5. Make a map of safe areas for another class. Give them the map, and explain why it is important to know these areas.

points ___ / 2

Find Test 5 Study Page

Glossary

4.1 Key Words Unit 1

classify – *v*, to arrange in classes

organism – *n*, a living thing

component – *n*, any of the parts that make up a complete system

habitat – *n*, a place where a plant or an animal lives naturally

measure – *n*, an action taken to ensure a specific outcome

adapt – *v*, to make or become suitable for different situations

prohibited – *adj*, something that is forbidden by law or rule

4.2 Key Words Unit 2

voluntary – *adj*, controlled by the mind done with thought

involuntary – *adj*, done without thought, not deliberate

expand – *v*, to make larger or increase

contract – *v*, to make shorter or smaller

exercise – *n*, an activity carried out to keep the body fit and healthy

protect – *v*, to shield from harm or keep safe; to defend

support – *v*, to bear the weight of; to hold up

4.3 Key Words Unit 3

magnitude – *n*, the extent or size of something

mass – *n*, the total amount of matter that a body contains—not affected by the force of gravity

volume – *n*, the amount of space that something occupies

fixed – *adj*, fastened securely in one place or position

pipette – *n*, a tube with a bulb at one end used for transferring or measuring liquids

test tube – *n*, a narrow glass tube that is used in laboratory experiments and tests

4.4 Key Words Unit 4

trajectory – *n*, the path of a moving object

displacement – *n*, the moving of something from its place or position

attract – *v*, to make something come closer

repel – *v*, to drive away by force

weight – *n*, a measure of how heavy something is as a result of the force of gravity

interact – *v*, to act on or influence each other

4.5 Key Words Unit 5

external – *adj*, forming the outside part of something

internal – *adj*, of or found on the inside of something

promote – *v*, to help something develop

produce – *v*, to bring into being in some way; to make or create

layer – *n*, a thickness or level of some material laid over an area

A

abiotic – *adj,* not from a living thing

adapt – *v*, to change to make suitable for a different situation—something changed in this way is an **adaptation**

adequate – *adj*, suitable; as it should be

alcoholism – *n*, a disease defined by an addiction to alcohol

alter – *v*, to make or become different; to change

articulation – *n*, an area where two bones are connected so that body parts can move, also called a joint

ash – *n*, the powdery substance that remains when something is burned

asthenosphere – *n*, a zone of the earth's mantle, beneath the lithosphere

atmosphere – *n*, the layer of air surrounding the earth

B

balance – *n*, a feeling of being steady or secure

beak – *n*, the hard, pointed part of the mouth of a bird or turtle

biome – *n*, a major habitat, classified according to vegetation and characterized by the adaptations of the living things that inhabit it

biotic – *adj,* of or relating to living things

birth defect – *n*, physical abnormality present at birth

bone – *n*, one of the hard parts that makes up the skeleton of a human or an animal—bones support the body and protect internal organs

C

Celsius – *n*, a scale and unit of measurement for temperature, also known as centigrade

central nervous system – *n*, a part of the nervous system that integrates incoming information and coordinates the activity of all body parts

community – *n*, a group of different kinds of plants or animals that live together in a certain area and relate to or depend on each other in some way

compete – *v*, to take part in a contest

compress – *v*, to force into a smaller space

condensation – *n*, the process by which a gas or vapor becomes a liquid

constant – *adj*, staying the same, continuing

consume – *v*, to eat or drink; to use up

core – *n*, the innermost region or center of the earth

crater – *n*, a large, bowl-shaped hollow in a flat surface, such as those created on the surface of the earth by meteors

crop – *n*, a plant that people grow on farms, mainly for food

crust – *n*, the solid outer part of the earth

curve – *n*, a gradually bending line, such as part of the edge of a circle

D

deciduous – *adj*, describing a plant or tree that loses its leaves in the fall and grows them back in the spring

decompose – *v*, to decay or rot

decrease – *v*, to become smaller in size or quantity

deposition – *n*, the change in state from a gas to a solid without an intermediate liquid phase

depression – *n*, a shallow hole; a hollow

direction – *n*, a line along which something moves, lies, faces or points

displace – *v*, to take the place of; to move something from its usual place

drug – *n*, a type of substance that has a very strong effect on the body, mind and feelings, and that can often make a person become addicted

E

ecosystem – *n*, all the living and nonliving things in an environment and the interactions between them

elastic – *adj*, able to expand and contract and be pushed in and out of shape

electric charge – *n*, a negative, positive or neutral charge found in the particles that make up all known matter

elongated – *adj*, unusually long in relation to its width; made longer

endure – *v*, to continue to exist over time; to put up with something bad or unpleasant

epicenter – *n*, the point on the earth's surface vertically above the origin point, or hypocenter, of an earthquake

equilibrium – *n*, the state in which opposing forces are balanced; a state of physical balance

exert – *v*, to apply; to put to use a force, influence or quality

expand – *v*, to make larger; to increase

exploit – *v*, to put to full use

F

feed – *v*, to take in as food; to give food to

fertile – *adj*, able to produce vegetation, crops or young easily

flex – *v*, to bend a part of the body

flow – *v*, to move along in a steady stream; to fall freely or loosely

food chain – *n*, a representation of the predator–prey relationships between different species in a habitat

force – *n*, the pulling or pushing effect that something has on something else

friction – *n*, the force of a substance that causes an object moving over it to slow down

fusion – *n*, the act or process of melting or combining

G

gas – *n*, a substance such as air that is not solid or liquid at normal temperatures and can move about freely and fill any available space

geosphere – *n*, the solid part of the earth composed of the crust and upper mantle

grind – *v*, to crush or break something into small pieces using a machine or hard surface

H

heart attack – *n*, a sudden and painful stoppage of the heart

hemisphere – *n*, half of a sphere shaped object

hydrosphere – *n*, all the water on the earth's surface and in its atmosphere

hypocenter – *n*, the point of origin of an earthquake below the earth's surface

I

improve – *v*, to make better

impulsive – *adj*, inclined to act without planning or thinking; done or performed without proper planning

increase – *v*, to become larger in size or quantity

influence – *n*, a force that produces a change in someone or something else

initiative – *n*, the first step toward doing something; a plan or program

injury – *n*, damage to a part of the body

interference – *n*, unwanted involvement

J

joint – *n*, a point where two or more bones meet, an articulation

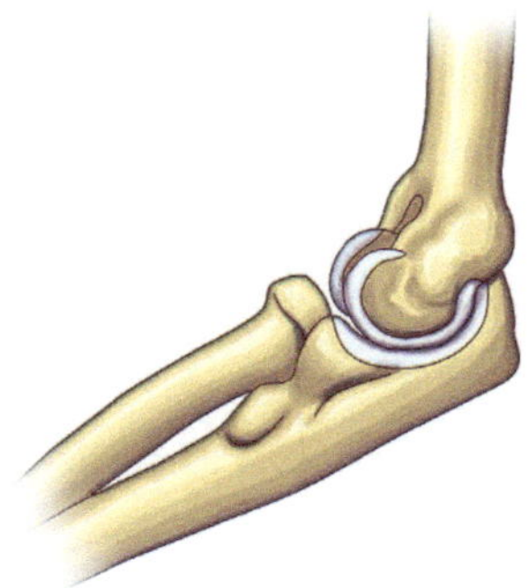

K

Kelvin scale – *n*, a thermodynamic temperature scale

knot – *n,* a unit of speed equivalent to 1.85 km/h and used especially in ships and airplanes

L

ligament – *n*, a strong, flexible band of tissue that connects bones or holds organs in place

limb – *n*, an arm, a leg or a wing

liquid – *n*, a substance that can be poured; a fluid that is not a gas

lithosphere – *n*, the most external layer of the earth made up of the oceanic crust, the continental crust and the exterior part of the mantle

logging – *n*, the cutting and processing trees into wood

lower – *v,* to move down

M

magma – *n*, very hot melted rock underneath the earth's surface—magma flows out of volcanoes as lava and then cools and forms into hard rock

magma chamber – *n*, a large underground pool of liquid rock beneath the earth's surface

magnet – *n,* a material that is able to attract certain metals

man-made – *adj,* created by humans, not natural

mantle – *n*, the region of the earth's interior between the crust and the core

measure – *v,* to find out the size or amount of something by using an instrument an action taken to ensure a specific outcome

meniscus – *n*, the curved upper surface of a liquid

mimicry – *n*, the skill or action of imitation; the close resemblance of an organism to another organism or inanimate object

mobility – *n*, the ability to move or be moved

molten – *adj*, made into a liquid by great heat, melted

motion – *n*, the act or process of changing place or moving

muscle – *n*, one of many tissues in the body that can contract and expand, making the body move

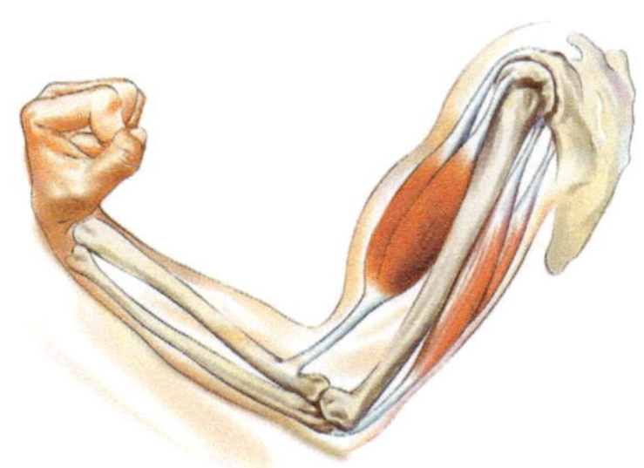

O

oppose – *v*, to resist or be against

organ – *n*, a part of a plant or an animal that does a particular job and is made up of different kinds of tissue

P

partially – *adv*, only in part, to a limited extent

particle – *n*, a very small piece; a body with volume or mass

paw – *n*, an animal's foot

pebble – *n*, a small, smooth, round stone

peripheral nervous system – *n*, a part of the nervous system including the nerves outside the brain and spinal cord whose function is to connect the central nervous system to the rest of the body

pillar – *n*, something that gives support or is an important part of something; a column that supports the roof of a building

pole – *n*, one end of the earth, the North or South Pole; the positive or negative end of a battery or magnet

pollen – *n*, the fine yellow powder produced by the male part of a flower

population – *n*, a group of people, animals or plants living in a place

porous – *adj*, having many tiny holes or spaces that allow water or air to pass through

predator – *n*, an animal that survives by eating other animals

preserve – *v*, to protect from damage, loss or decay

prey – *n*, an animal that is hunted and killed by another animal for food

process – *v*, to treat, prepare or convert something using a series of steps

prone – *adj*, likely to do, or be affected by, something

R

raise – *v,* to move up

reflex – *n,* an action done without conscious thought in response to stimuli

rigid – *adj,* stiff or unbending

S

scale – *n,* a weighing machine—it works by balancing the object being weighed against another weight or against the force of a spring

scarce – *adj,* difficult to find or obtain; rare

seismic – *adj,* relating to earthquakes, tremors or other movements of the earth's crust

shock – *n,* what is felt when an electric charge passes through the body

slightly – *adv,* to a small degree

solid – *n,* a substance that is not a liquid or gas and that has a fixed shape

solidification – *n,* the change in state from a liquid to a solid

species – *n,* a group of animals that share common characteristics—members of the same species can mate and have offspring

spine – *n,* a stiff, sharp point growing out of an animal or a plant

standstill – *n,* a state in which all activity or motion is stopped

state – *n,* the physical condition in which a substance can exist, either solid, liquid or gas

straight line – *n,* a line traveling in a constant direction; a line with no curvature or breaks

strengthen – *v,* to make stronger

sublimation – *n,* the transition of a solid to a gas stage with no intermediate liquid stage

succulent – *n,* a plant that has thick, fleshy leaves or stems adapted for storing water

T

tectonic plate – *n,* one of the huge, thick pieces of the earth's crust—there are seven major plates

tendon – *n,* a tough band or cord of tissue that attaches a muscle to a bone or other body part

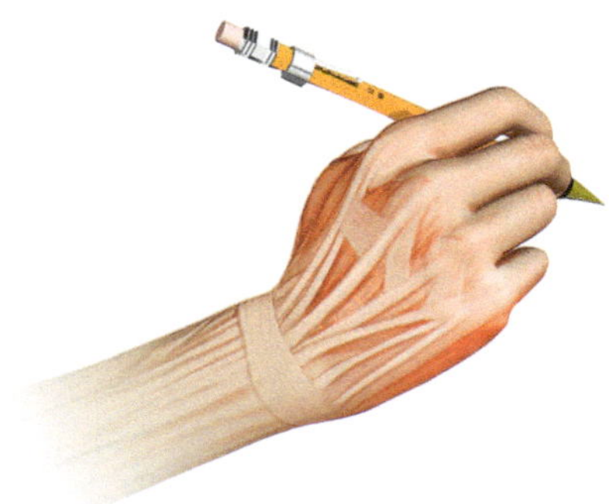

texture – *n,* the appearance and feel of the surface of something

thermometer – *n*, an instrument for measuring temperature

tremor – *n*, a shaking or trembling; a slight earthquake

tsunami – *n*, a huge wave caused by a volcanic eruption, an earthquake or a landslide

twig – *n*, a small, thin stick from a tree or bush

V

vapor – *n*, the gaseous state of water or another substance

vaporization – *n*, the change in state from a liquid to a gas

velocity – *n*, the speed at which an object is traveling in a particular direction

volcanic cone – *n*, a volcanic formation created by material pushed out from a volcanic vent and piling up around the vent in the shape of a cone with a central crater

W

webbed – *adj*, having or connected by a web

X

X-ray – *n*, a type of radiation that can penetrate solid substances that ordinary rays of light cannot, and that is used to take pictures of the inside of bodies

Cutout 1
Use on page 29 (**Unit 1**).

Cutout 2
Use on page 33 (**Unit 1**).

Cutouts

Cutout 3
Use on page 34 (**Unit 1**).

Cutout 4
Use on page 37 (**Unit 2**).

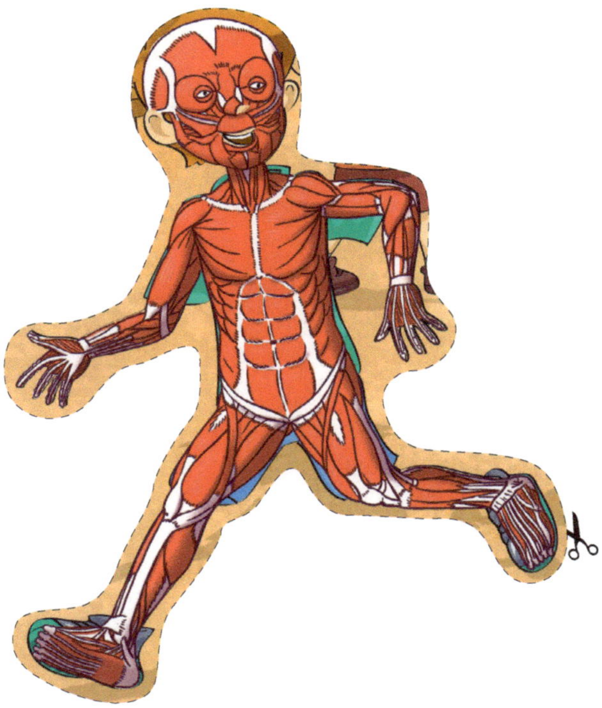
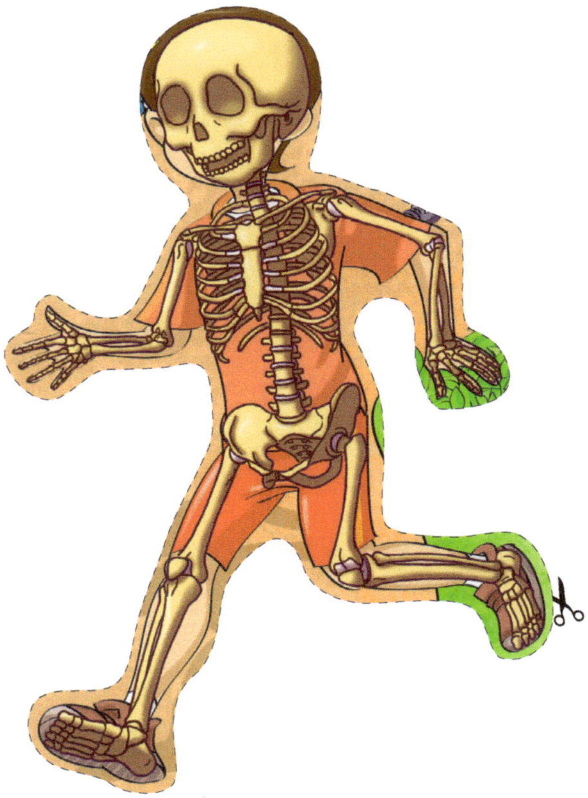

Cutout 5
Use on page 70 (**Unit 2**).

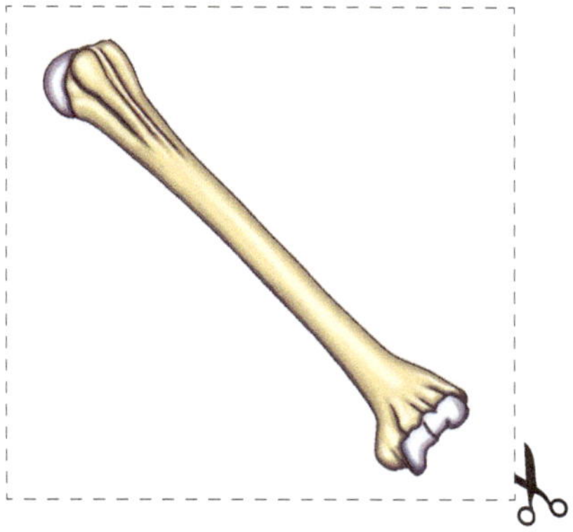

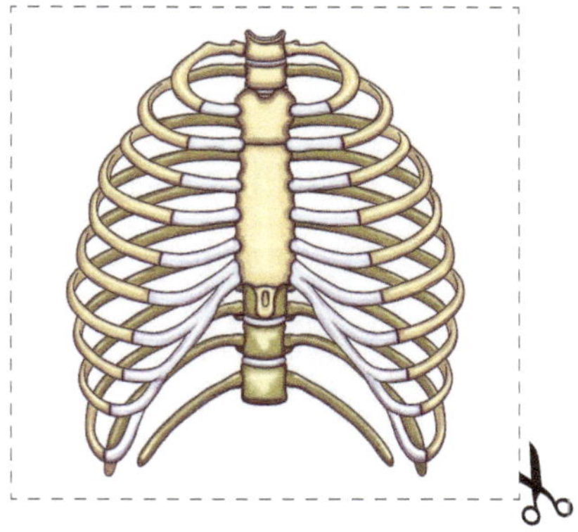

Cutout 6
Use on page 92 (**Unit 3**).

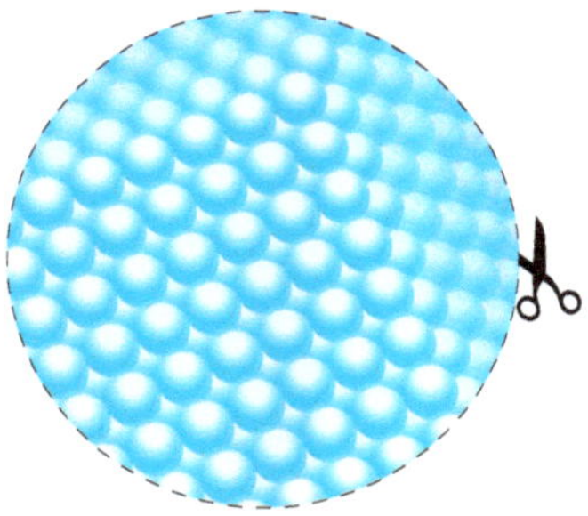

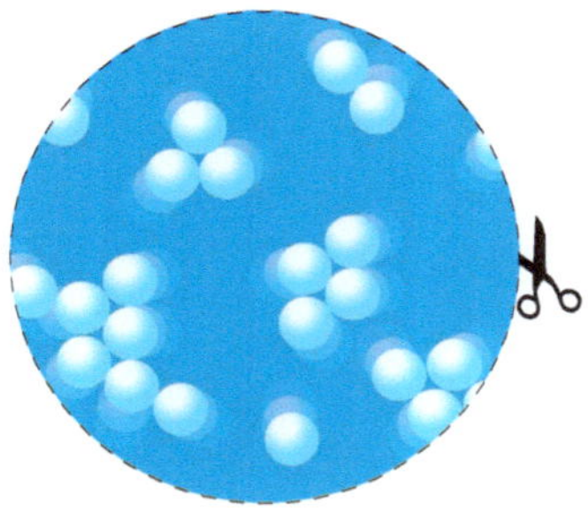

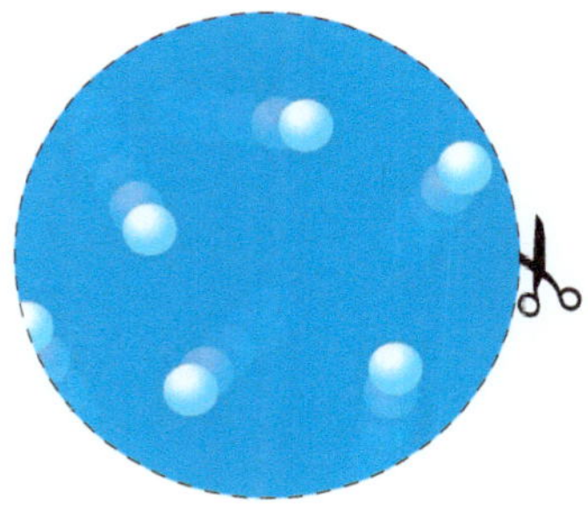

Cutout 7

Use on page 93 (**Unit 3**).

For question **a**.

stones

milk

air inside a balloon

For question **b**.

stones

milk

air inside a balloon

For question **c**.

stones

milk

air inside a balloon

Cutouts

Cutout 8

Use on page 128 (**Unit 4**).

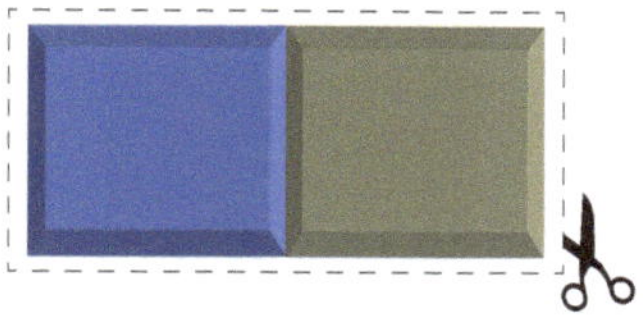
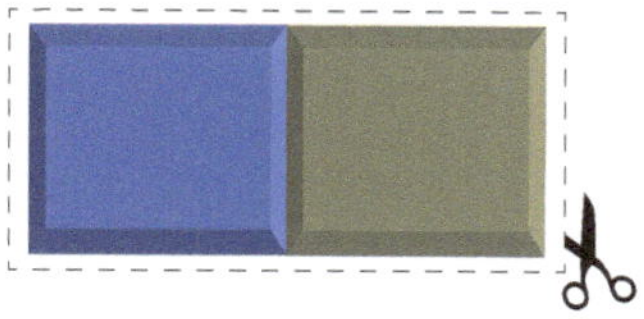
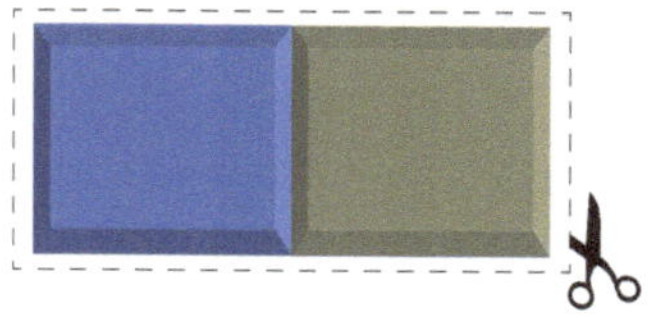
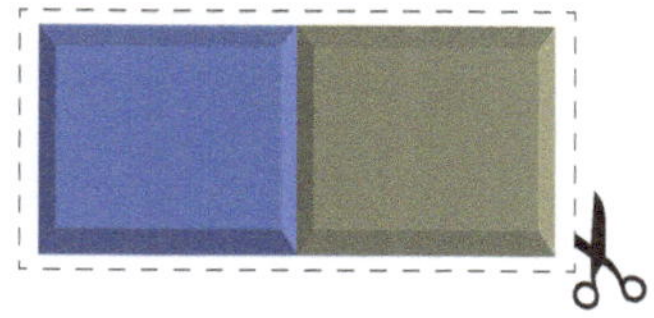

Cutout 9

Use on page 131 (**Unit 4**).

Cutout 10

Use on page 135 (**Unit 5**).

Activity Card 1

How Can I Make a Garden?

What Do I Need?

- a wooden box
- plastic wrap
- a small shovel and rake
- a watering can
- soil
- basil, parsley and cilantro seeds

Remember, always ask your parents for help!

What Do I Do?

1. Cover the inside of the box with plastic wrap. Use a pencil to poke some small holes in the plastic to let the water drain.
2. Fill the box with a thick layer of soil.
3. Using the rake, make lines in the soil. Put the seeds in, and cover them up with a little bit of soil.
4. Leave the garden in a sunny place.

Don't forget to water your garden!

Activity Card 2

How Can I Make Recycled Paper?

1. Collect the following materials: newspaper or used notebook paper, a pitcher, water, two large bowls, a wooden spoon, a frame with a screen, a strainer with small holes, fabric cut to the same size as the screen and two pieces of wood.
2. Cut the paper into small pieces and put it into the bowl. Add water and stir the mixture until it forms a pulp. Let the mixture set for a few hours.
3. Put the paper mixture in the strainer and then transfer it to a new bowl.
4. Use the spoon and your hands to make a paste.
5. Put the screen into the bowl until it is covered with the paper paste.
6. Let the water drain out.
7. Put one piece of fabric under the screen and another on top.
8. Then place the two pieces of wood on top of the fabric (one on each side) and push all the water out. Note: you can put a heavy object on top of the wood to help.
9. Place the piece of recycled paper in the sunlight to dry. Now you can draw on it!

Activity Card 3

Food Pyramid

Menu for a Balanced Diet

Breakfast	Lunch	Dinner

Activity Card 4

Food Handling Practices

Newton's Disk

Cut out the circle. Then put a pencil in the center and spin it.

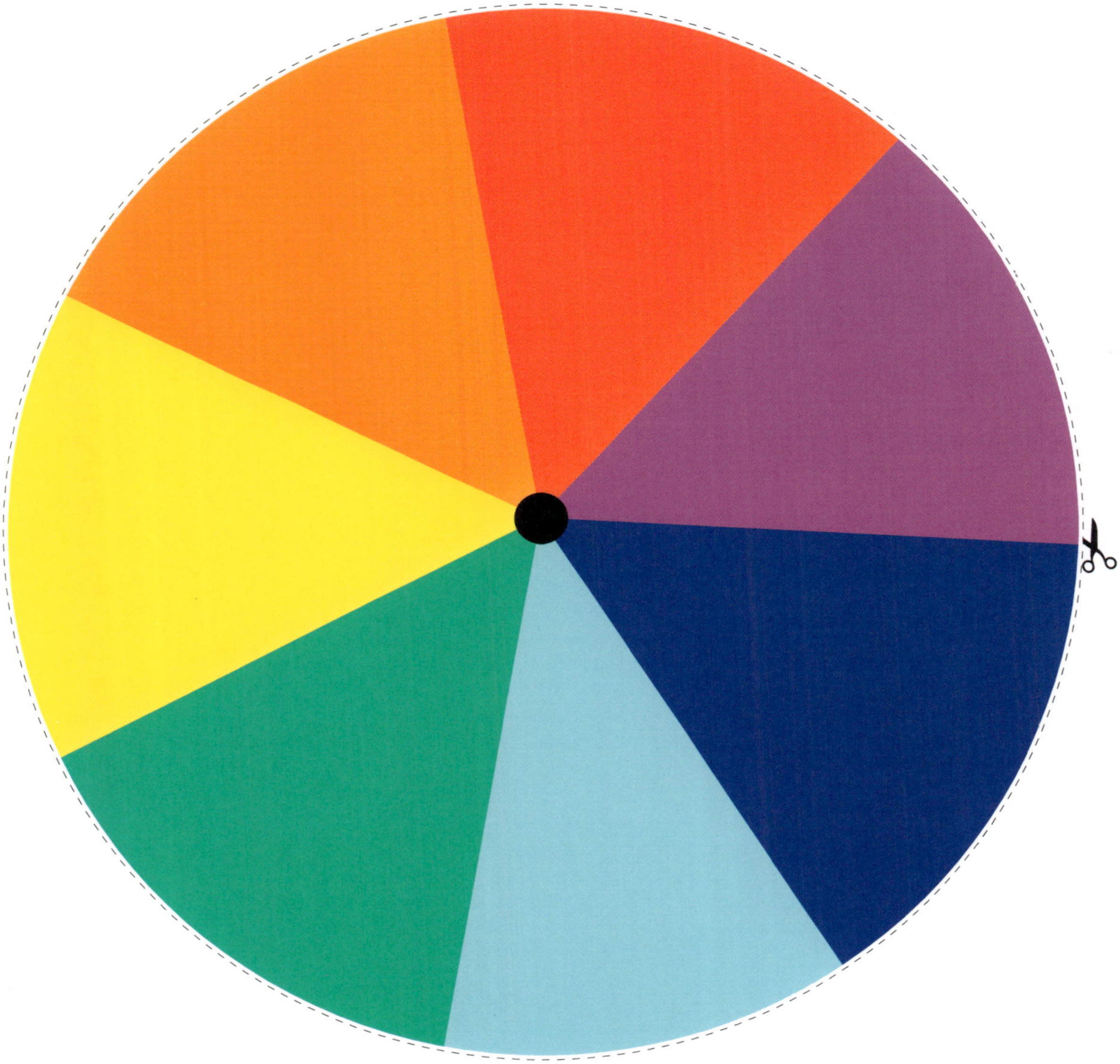

Constellations

Eclipses

Phases of the Moon

Test 1 Study Page • Summary

In nature, living things are organized into:

populations **communities** **ecosystems**

An ecosystem consists of two types of interacting components:

Biotic factors: all living things in an ecosystem, like plants and animals.

Abiotic factors: all nonliving things in an ecosystem, like air, water, rocks and temperature.

The biotic factors can interact in different ways, like competition, mutualism and predation.

Living things have developed adaptations in their structures and behavior.

movement	diet	protection
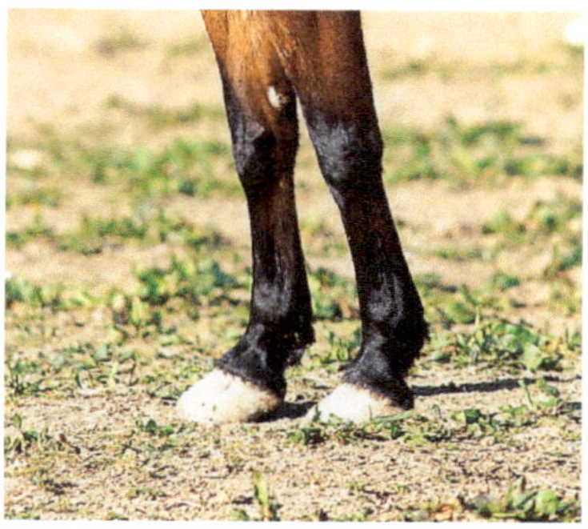		

Section 3

2. Read the following text and draw the corresponding food chain.
The red fox lives throughout the northern hemisphere. It is an animal that feeds mainly on meat and therefore hunts different types of smaller animals, including some small birds. The house wren is a small bird that shares the ecosystem with the red fox and feeds on different types of insects, including herbivorous insects.

3. What negative effects can human activity have on ecosystems?

4. Name three protection measures for ecosystems in your country.

glue here

glue here

glue here

glue here

glue here

Test 1 Study Page • Review

Remove, answer, and glue in your notebook.

Sections 1 and 2

1. Look at the picture.

a. Write the biotic and abiotic components in the table.

Biotic Components	
Abiotic Components	

b. What interactions are shown in the picture?

____

____

c. Which living thing in the picture does not possess the adaptations necessary to survive in this ecosystem?

____

Name: ______________________________ Grade: __________

The living things in an ecosystem can be classified in three groups:

Producers use the energy from sunlight and other environmental substances to produce their food.
Consumers obtain their energy by feeding on other living things.
Decomposers transform the remains and waste left by other organisms.

Producers, consumers and decomposers are all related to each other by their diets. These relationships are represented in food chains.

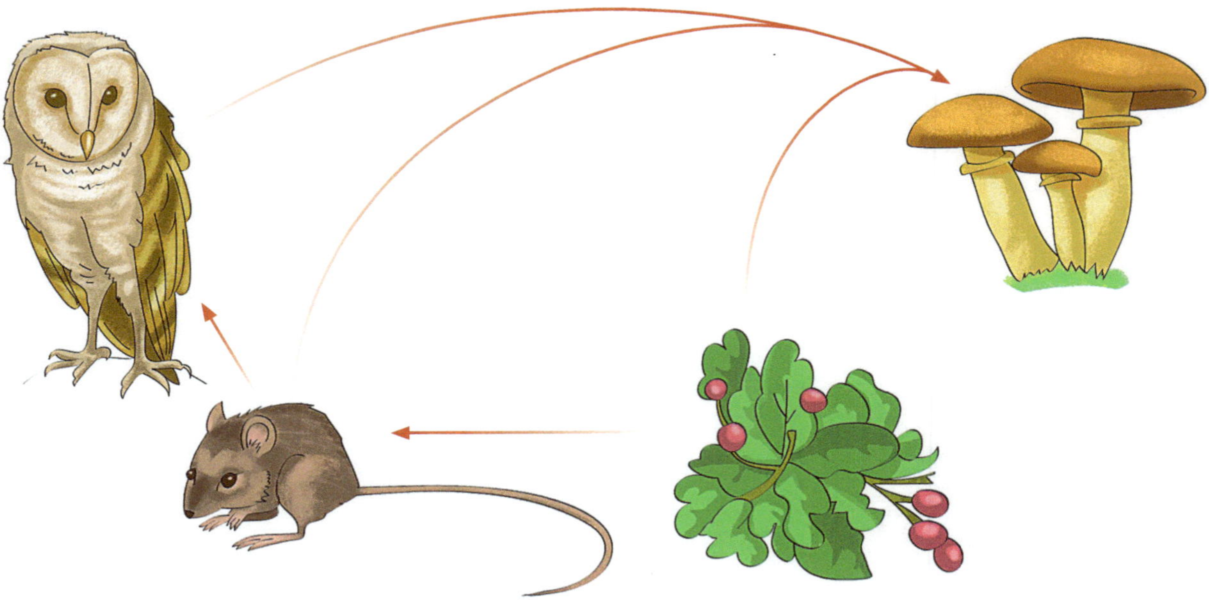

Different **human activities alter ecosystems** and sometimes irreparably damage the environment.

There are different initiatives that seek to protect and preserve the ecosystems of our planet. For example:

- Protect wild areas.
- Prohibit hunting in certain areas or seasons.
- Dispose of garbage and trash correctly.

Test 2 Study Page • Summary

The **skeletal system** supports the body. It also protects certain organs and allows movement. It consists of bones and joints.

Some of the principal bones in the body are:

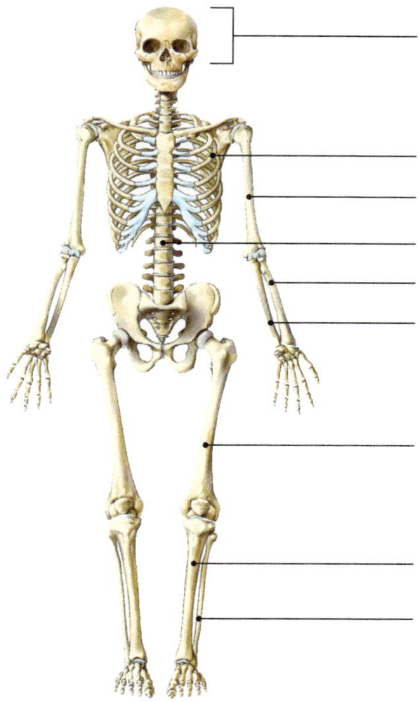

The **muscular system** consists of muscles and tendons. Muscles contract and expand to make the body move. Tendons connect the muscles to bones. Movable joints allow muscles and bones to interact, producing all the movements of the body.

The skeletal system and muscular system together are called the **musculoskeletal system**. It is important to exercise to keep this system healthy. Some of the principal muscles are:

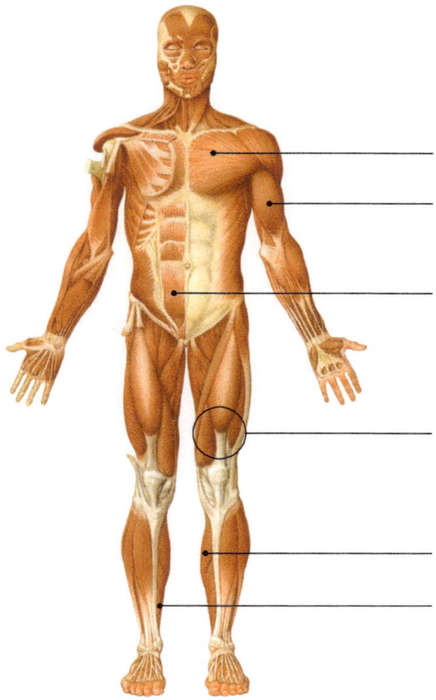

Section 3

5. Write the part of the nervous system that corresponds to each description.

- It controls breathing, blood circulation and some eye movements. → ______
- It sends information to and from the nervous system organs in the cranium. → ______
- It coordinates muscles, posture and balance. → ______
- They are in all parts of the body, sending and receiving information. → ______
- It controls functions like thought and memory. → ______

Section 4

6. Mark the parts of the body that are affected by consuming alcohol.

- ☐ heart
- ☐ brain
- ☐ skin
- ☐ liver
- ☐ hair
- ☐ stomach
- ☐ bones
- ☐ pancreas
- ☐ fingernails

glue here

glue here

glue here

glue here

glue here

Test 2 Study Page • Review

Remove, answer, and glue in your notebook.

Section 1

1. Find seven bones in the word search.

R	A	D	I	U	S	G	F	E	M	U	R
R	Q	E	H	J	U	M	Z	H	P	L	M
A	S	R	I	V	R	C	L	W	Y	N	O
B	V	E	R	T	E	B	R	A	E	A	G
T	L	F	A	N	M	U	E	R	S	P	H
K	I	E	X	B	U	M	A	L	B	F	D
S	Y	B	D	J	H	W	C	R	I	B	S
X	I	Q	I	F	M	U	L	G	T	S	V
P	D	A	N	A	S	H	W	K	B	C	R

2. What are the functions of the skeletal system?

Section 2

3. If you pick up a book with your hand, how does your arm move? Explain, considering the function of each of the arm's parts.

4. What are the benefits of physical activity for the musculoskeletal system?

Name: ______________________________ Grade: __________

The **nervous system** is in charge of receiving and interpreting information and controlling bodily responses. It consists of:

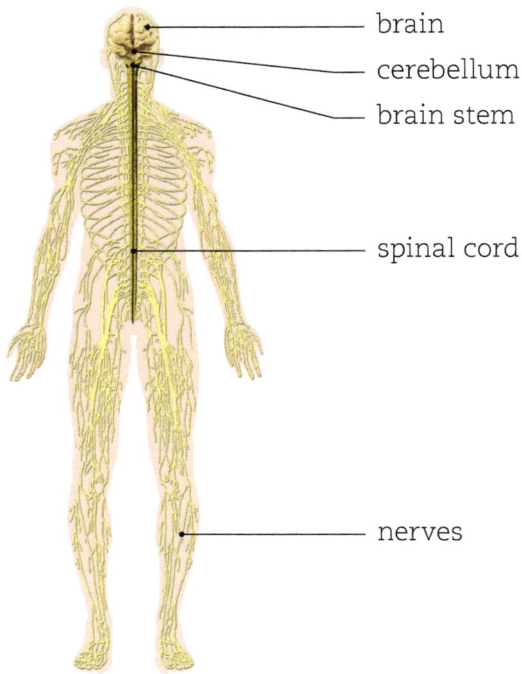

Alcohol is a substance found in alcoholic beverages. It is considered a drug because it alters the normal functions of the body when it is consumed. Alcohol can cause addiction in addition to having harmful effects on bodily organs, especially those shown in the image.

To avoid alcohol, you can do the following:

- Promote open communication within the family.
- Play sports and do exercise in your free time.
- Get together with friends to eat and drink healthy products.
- Learn about the harmful effects of alcohol.

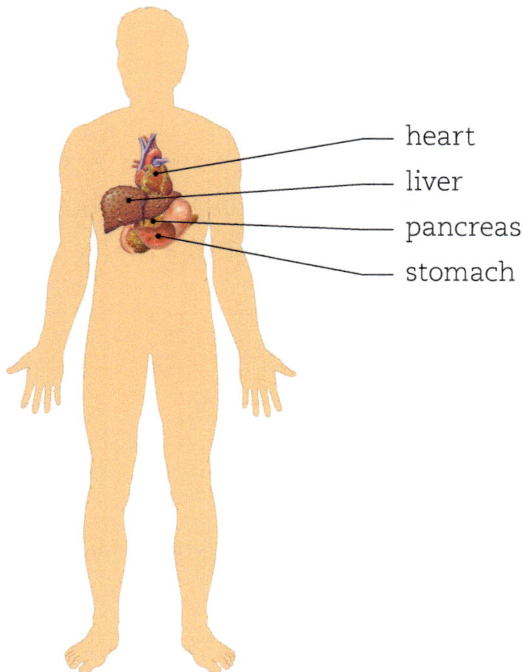

Test 3 Study Page • Summary

Everything around us consists of matter.

Matter

is characterized by:

- having mass
- having volume (it occupies space)
- being naturally found in different states, such as solid, liquid and gas

Solids, liquids and gases have different characteristics, as seen in the table below.

	Solid	Liquid	Gas
Maintains its shape	✓		
Has constant volume	✓	✓	
Adapts easily to the container it is in		✓	✓
Can be compressed			✓
Can expand			✓
Can flow		✓	✓
Particles are	tightly packed	slightly packed	separated

Section 3

3. Find five measuring instruments and five units of measurement.

D	R	O	P	P	E	R	T	G	S	D
D	W	E	Y	I	L	H	H	S	C	E
O	K	P	A	V	B	M	E	F	A	G
P	I	P	E	T	T	E	R	L	L	R
G	L	V	C	F	P	O	M	T	E	E
Q	O	J	D	E	O	Z	O	X	A	E
F	G	R	C	M	A	W	M	S	P	S
Y	R	E	B	U	L	K	E	K	Y	C
P	A	I	R	L	L	I	T	E	R	E
D	M	S	C	N	R	G	E	L	F	L
Y	U	B	M	Q	M	S	R	V	H	S
C	Y	L	I	N	D	E	R	I	P	I
I	X	B	U	G	A	S	C	N	S	U
B	R	A	I	Z	Q	K	L	S	U	S
G	R	A	M	S	J	S	P	D	Y	A

4. Classify the instruments and units of measurement in the word search according to the properties that they measure.

Instruments		
Mass	Volume	Temperature

Units of Measurement		
Mass	Volume	Temperature

glue here

glue here

glue here

glue here

glue here

Test 3 Study Page • Review

Remove, answer, and glue in your notebook.

Section 1

1. Define the following concepts:

Matter: ______________________________

____

Mass: ______________________________

____

Volume: ______________________________

____

Section 2

2. Write the state of each circled object. Then describe the characteristics of each state.

	Physical State	Characteristics

Name: ______________________________ Grade: ____________

Matter can also change from one state to another (change in state) when the temperature increases and decreases.

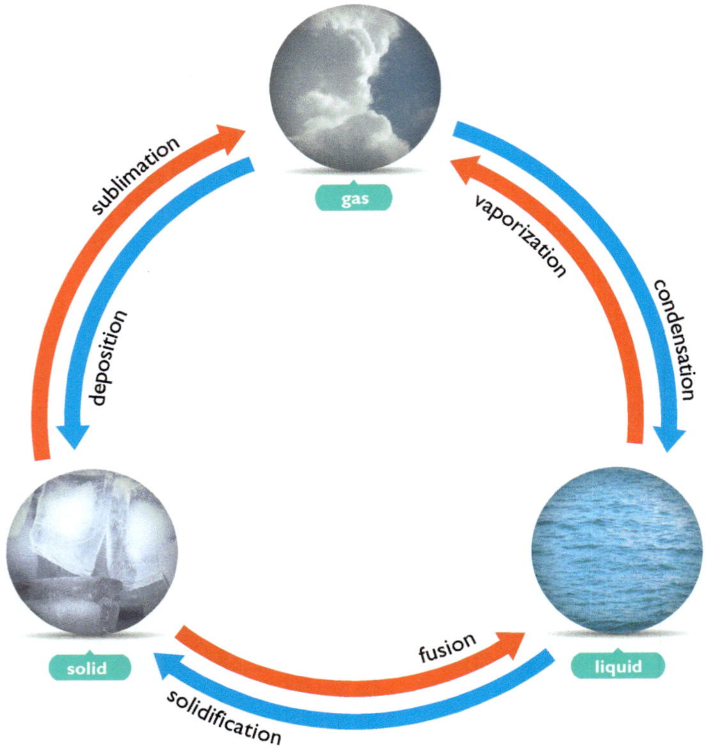

Mass, volume and temperature can be measured for every type of body.

	Measuring Instruments	Units of Measurement
Mass	scales	kilogram (kg) / grams (g)
Volume	graduated material (pipettes, cylinders, flasks, droppers, etc.)	liter (l) / milliliters (ml)
Temperature	thermometer	Kelvin (K) / Degrees Celsius (°C)

Test 4 Study Page • Summary

Motion is defined as the change in position of a body—in other words, when a body changes its location in relation to a point of reference.

Some concepts that characterize movement are:

Trajectory	Displacement	Speed
This is the path a body travels along when it is in motion.	This corresponds to the straight line connecting the initial position of a body with its final position after movement.	This relates the distance a body has traveled to the time it takes to do so. Speed is calculated using this equation: $$\text{speed} = \frac{\text{distance}}{\text{time}}$$

Force is an interaction between two bodies. One body exerts force and another receives force. Forces can be classified as:

Contact Forces	Noncontact Forces
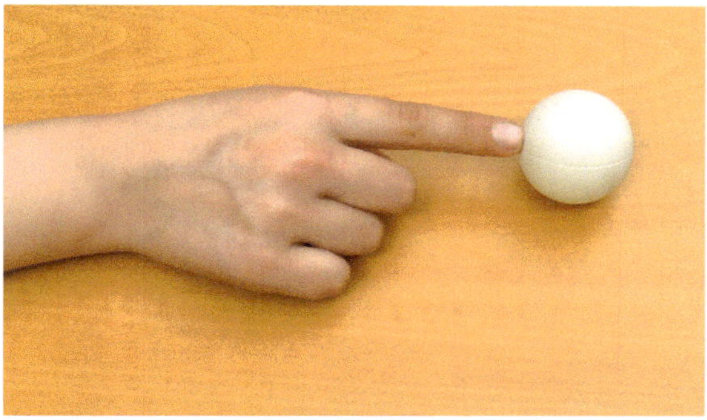	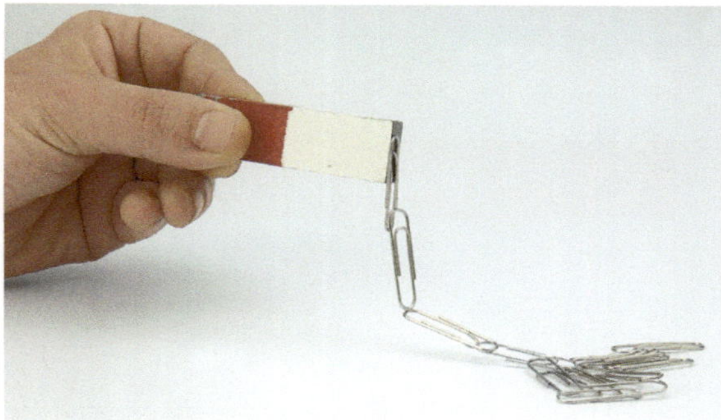

Section 3

5. Look at the images and respond.

situation 1

situation 2

In which case would it be more difficult to move the pencil case? Explain why.

____

____

6. Give an example from your daily life in which each of these forces can be seen.

Frictional Force	Gravitational Force
Magnetic Force	**Electric Force**

Test 4 Study Page • Review

Remove, answer, and glue in your notebook.

Section 1

1. Define the following concepts. Give one example of each.

Concept	Definition	Example
Trajectory		
Motion		
Speed		
Force		

2. Calculate the speed of a body whose motion is shown below.

Time (seconds)	Distance (meters)
2	4

Section 2

3. When you open a door, what is exerting force and what is receiving force?

____

4. Mark wants to wash his soccer ball, so he puts it on the ground. When he sprays it with the hose, the water moves the ball. Why does it move? Explain.

____

____

Name: ________________________________ Grade: ____________

The application of force can cause different effects. For example:

Change in Shape | Change in Direction | Change in Speed

Types of Force

Frictional Force is the force that opposes a body's motion. It depends on the mass and characteristics of the bodies in contact.

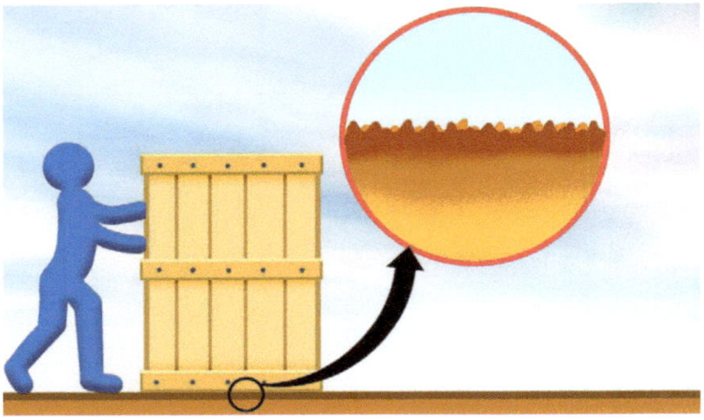

Gravitational Force, or weight, is the force with which the earth or another celestial body attracts objects to its surface.

Magnetic Force is the interaction of attraction or repulsion between magnets.

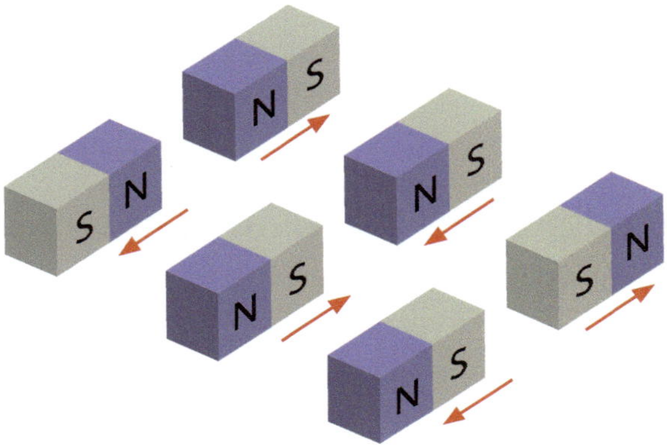

Electric Force is the interaction of attraction or repulsion between two electrically charged bodies.

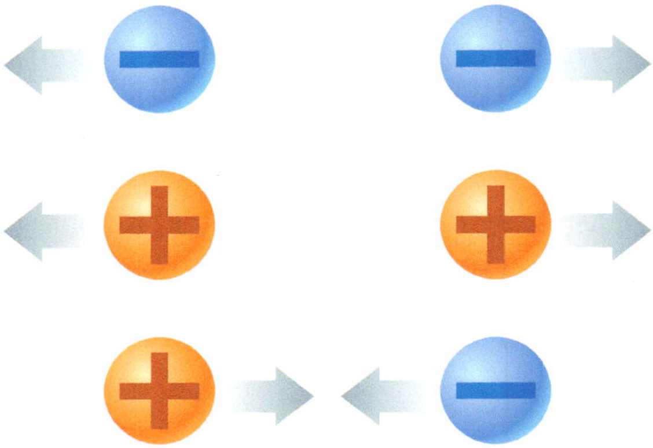

Test 5 Study Page • Summary

The earth consists of three major components:

atmosphere **hydrosphere** **geosphere**

The geosphere is the rocky part of the earth, but it is not just what we see on the exterior. It consists of three layers:

The crust is the most external layer of the earth. It forms the continents, mountains and the ocean floor. It is the thinnest layer and has the lowest temperature.

The mantle is the layer following the crust. It is 2,900 kilometers thick. Its temperature can be up to 3,000 °C. The asthenosphere is a liquid area of the mantle near the crust.

The core is the deepest layer. It is 3,500 kilometers thick, and its temperature reaches 6,000 °C. The inner core is solid, and the outer core is liquid.

Section 2

3. Match each concept with the correct description.

Tectonic plates	Exact point where a tremor originates.
Lithosphere	Point on the surface of the earth located directly above the hypocenter.
Earthquake	Movement on the surface of the earth due to the tectonic plates in the lithosphere.
Tsunami	Giant wave that can occur after a tremor in the oceanic crust.
Hypocenter	Upper part of the earth consisting of the crust and the upper part of the mantle.
Epicenter	Group of plates forming the lithosphere.

glue here

glue here

glue here

glue here

glue here

Test 5 Study Page • Review

Remove, answer, and glue in your notebook.

Section 1

1. Complete the diagram.

2. Describe each layer of the earth.

Crust: ______________________________

____

____

Mantle: ______________________________

____

____

Core: ______________________________

____

____

Name: ______________________________ Grade: __________

The lithosphere is the external layer of the earth. It consists of the crust and the u[p]
part of the mantle. It is divided into tectonic plates.

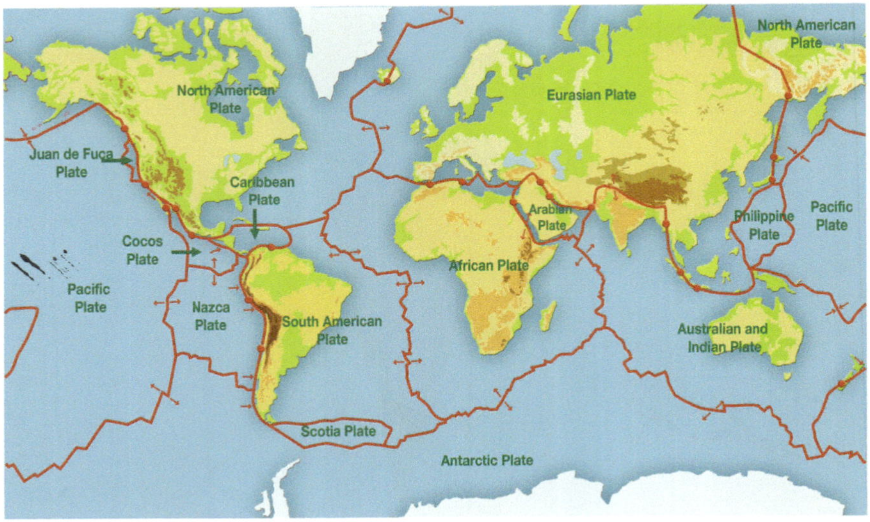

The tectonic plates of the lithosphere move in different ways, which creates natural phenomena such as tremors, tsunamis and volcanoes.

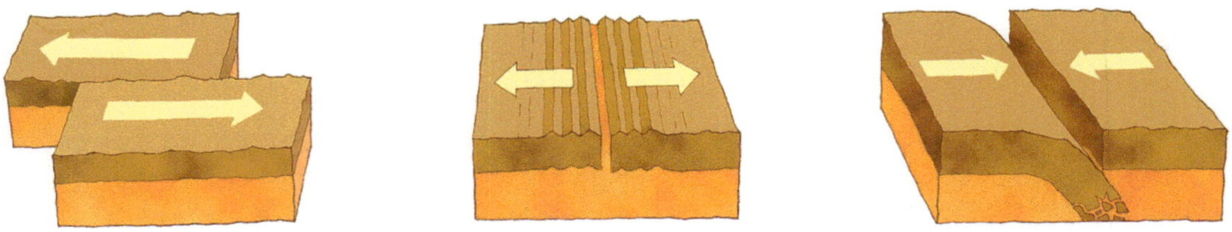

The movements of the lithosphere can cause natural disasters that seriously affect human beings, so it is important that each person is informed and prepared to act in any emergency.

In case of an emergency, it is important to:

- Identify risks.
- Stay calm.
- Not act impulsively.
- Pay attention to the information given by the authorities.

Test 1 Study Page • Summary

Plant Structures and Their Functions

Roots absorb water and minerals and give stability to plants.

The **stem** transports water and minerals to all the structures of the plant. It also connects the roots with the leaves, flowers and fruits.

Leaves, through photosynthesis, produce the necessary nutrients for the plant.

Life Cycle and Reproduction of Plants

Germination: When the fruit falls, it releases the seeds. Under the right conditions, the seeds will germinate and produce a new plant.

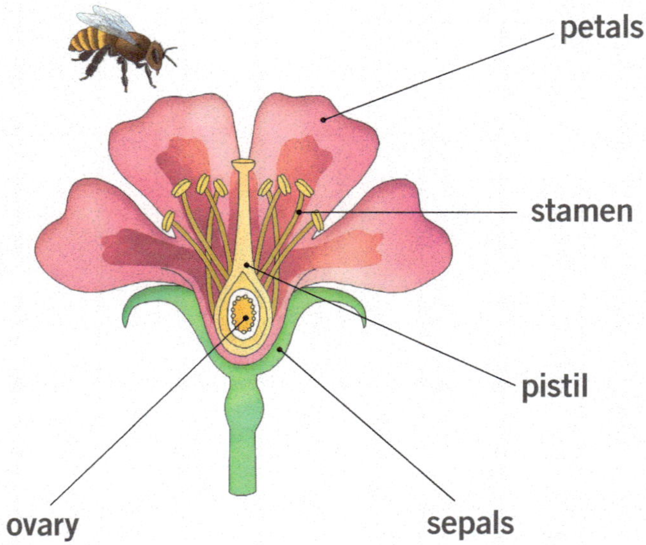

Pollination: This is the way plants reproduce. It occurs when pollen is transferred from the stamen to the pistil.

Fruit formation: In the ovary, the pollen fertilizes the eggs and they become seeds. The ovary grows until it covers the seeds, forming the fruit.

Section 3

3. Color each box using the key.

- (orange) It benefits other living things.
- (blue) It benefits human beings.
- (green) It benefits the environment.

☐ A bird builds its nest in a tree.

☐ A woman drinks chamomile tea.

☐ Trees stop a flood.

☐ A girl is eating an apple.

☐ Animals are eating leaves.

glue here

glue here

glue here

glue here

glue here

Test 1 Study Page • Review

Remove, answer, and glue in your notebook.

Section 1

1. Match the main plant structures with their functions.

Roots	Transports water and minerals to all the other parts of the plant.
Stem	Give stability and absorb water and minerals.
Leaves	Make nutrients through the process of photosynthesis.

Section 2

2. Answer **T** for true or **F** for false. If the statement is false, explain why.

a. ________ Seeds can germinate in all weather conditions.

____

b. ________ The ovary gets thicker to produce the fruit and the stem.

____

c. ________ Pollinators help in the process of pollination.

____

d. ________ Germination results in a new plant.

____

Name: ______________________________ Grade: __________

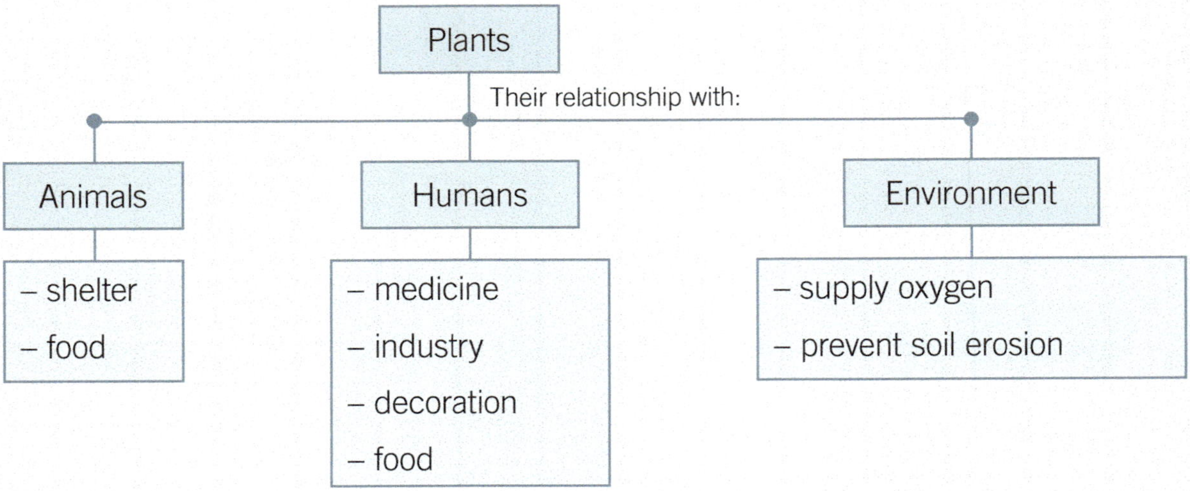

Types of Plants

Native Plants	Exotic Plants
These reproduce and grow naturally in a particular region—for instance, the giant redwood in California.	These have been introduced by humans—for instance, the eucalyptus from Australia to many parts of the Americas.

- Plants that can be used for medical purposes include mint, lavender, chamomile, ginger and aloe vera.
- Plant products used in industry include cotton and wood.
- Principal food crops include nuts, vegetables, fruits and grains.

Test 2 Study Page • Summary

Natural Resources

- can be classified as:
  - renewable
  - nonrenewable
- can originate from:
  - animals
  - minerals
  - plants

Artificial Resources

Types of Natural Resources

- mining
- forestry
- agricultural
- livestock
- water
- fishing

Section 2

4. Propose two measures to conserve or protect natural resources. Explain.

First measure: ______________________________

____

Second measure: ______________________________

____

5. Which objects are recyclable?

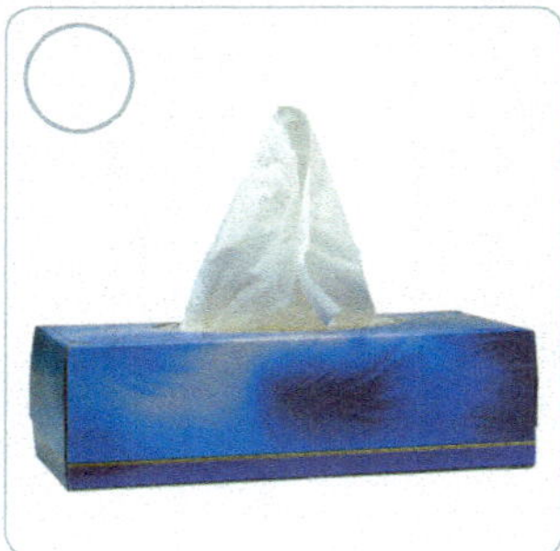

6. What could you make with soda can tabs? Explain.

____

____

glue here
glue here
glue here
glue here
glue here

Test 2 Study Page • Review

Remove, answer, and glue in your notebook.

Section 1

1. Which of these natural resources is **non**renewable?

- [ ] sheep
- [ ] oil
- [ ] trees

2. What are artificial resources?

____

____

3. Draw lines connecting the waste with the correct containers.

egg shells

plastic container

glass bottle

orange peel

Name: ______________________________ Grade: __________

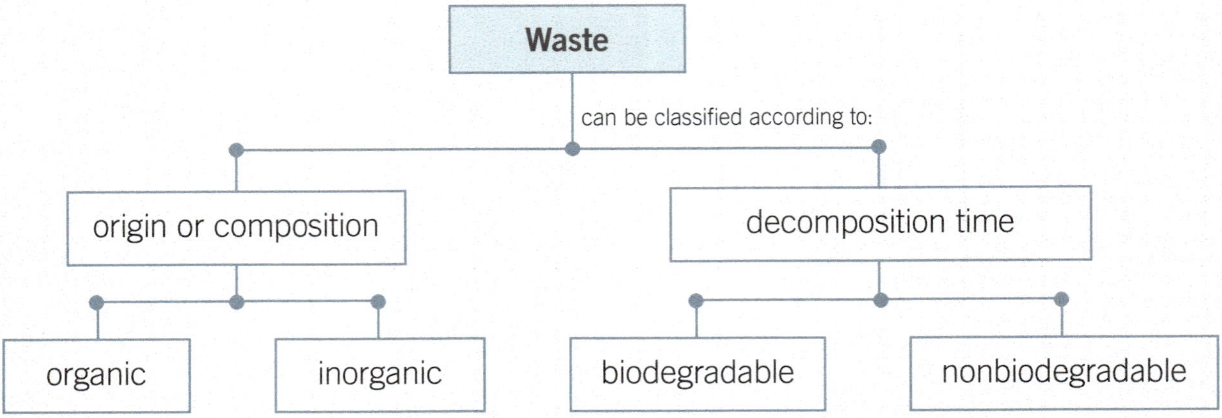

Some measures to preserve resources are:

– Plant new trees and take care of plants.
– Turn off the tap when you are not using water.
– Turn off lights when you do not need them on.

Recycling	Reusing	Reducing
In this process, waste is converted into reusable material. New objects can be made with this recycled material.	This is to lower the amount of waste by using objects as many times as possible. Then less garbage is produced, and fewer resources are used to make new objects.	This is to lower the amount of waste by decreasing the number of things we buy in order to save renewable natural resources.

Some actions that help reduce waste are:

– Avoid using plastic bags; instead, use paper bags or reusable bags.
– Use reusable bottles.
– Use rechargeable batteries.

Test 3 Study Page • Summary

Foods

plant origin

animal origin

A Balanced Diet

In order for the body to be **healthy**, it is necessary to have a **balanced diet**. It is best to maintain **healthy eating habits** by eating things that benefit the body, like vegetables, fruits, low-fat meats and milk.

Eating a lot of unhealthy food can harm the body.

Foods

healthy

unhealthy

Section 2

3. Suggest three good hygiene practices for handling food during lunchtime at school.

1: ______________________________

2: ______________________________

3: ______________________________

4. Illustrate the good practices from the previous activity.

5. You have just made plans to make and eat a healthy lunch all week. Have you ever done this before?

____

____

glue here

glue here

glue here

glue here

glue here

Test 3 Study Page • Review

Remove, complete, and glue in your notebook.

Section 1

1. Complete the diagram with examples.

Healthy Foods	→	______ ______ ______	→	Why are they healthy? ______ ______ ______
Unhealthy Foods	→	______ ______ ______	→	Why are they unhealthy? ______ ______ ______

2. Propose a healthy lunch that you can bring to school for each day of the week.

Monday	Tuesday	Wednesday	Thursday	Friday

Name: ______________________________ Grade: __________

Food Handling

Some recommendations to avoid contracting food-related illnesses are:

- Always wash your hands with soap and water before eating.
- Wash fruits well before eating them.
- Wash vegetables under running water, and with some, like lettuce, make sure to throw away the outside leaves.
- Before peeling fruits or vegetables, you also need to wash them.
- Only use water, not soap or detergent, to wash fruits and vegetables.
- Certain fruits, like strawberries, need to be washed carefully because they grow close to the ground.
- Keep cooking areas clean.
- Keep animals away from cooking areas.
- Make sure fruits and vegetables are fresh, not moldy.
- Keep foods that need to be refrigerated in the refrigerator.

Do not buy canned foods that are dented, foods in plastic wrap with holes, foods that have a bad smell or strange color, or products that have expired.

Some illnesses that you can contract from poor food handling and preparation are: gastroenteritis, cholera and typhoid fever.

Test 4 Study Page • Summary

Objects that emit light are called **luminous bodies**. The sun, lightbulbs and stars are all **luminous bodies**.
Objects that are lit up by luminous bodies are called **illuminated bodies**. A table, your pencil case and your pencils are illuminated bodies.

There are **natural** and **artificial** light sources.

Natural light sources emit light and are found in nature. Some examples are the sun, stars and some insects like glowworms and fireflies.	**Artificial light sources** are man-made. Some examples are lightbulbs, candles and matches.

Light travels in a straight line and also **propagates** or **spreads out in all directions**.

We can see clearly through **transparent objects**. Light passes completely though them.	Light passes through **translucent objects,** but we cannot see through them clearly. Light does not pass through them completely.	We cannot see through **opaque objects.** Light does not pass through them.

When an opaque object stops the passage of light, it creates a dark zone called a **shadow**.

4. Explain why the chair has a shadow.

____

____

____

____

5. Write the corresponding light phenomenon below each picture.

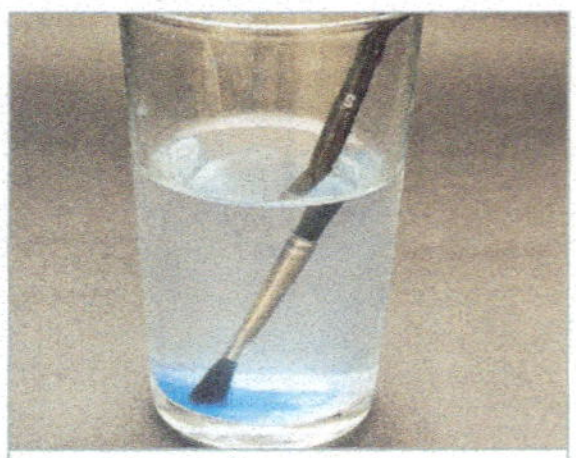

Section 3

6. Complete the sentences.

Sound is produced by the ______________________ of an object.

Sound travels in all ______________________.

The characteristic that allows us to classify loud and soft sounds is ______________________. Tone is the characteristic that allows us to classify ______________ and ______________ sounds.

Absorption and ______________________ are phenomena that happen to sound.

Test 4 Study Page • Review

Remove, answer, and glue in your notebook.

Section 1

1. Identify the luminous bodies with an **L**.
Identify the illuminated bodies with an **I**.

2. Which activities would you do using natural light and which would you do using artificial light? Give two examples.

Activities Done with Light	
Natural	Artificial

Section 2

3. Look around you and complete the table with examples.

Types of Objects		
transparent	translucent	opaque

Name: ______________________________ Grade: __________

Light can experience the following phenomena:

Reflection

Refraction

Dispersion

Sound is produced by the vibration of an object. Sound **travels in all directions** and **through different mediums**.

Sound intensity is the characteristic that allows us to classify sounds as loud or soft. **Tone** is the characteristic that allows us to classify sounds as deep or high-pitched.

Sound can be **reflected** and **absorbed**.

When sound passes from one medium to another, some of the sound is absorbed.	When sound is reflected, it generally changes direction and loses energy—in other words, its intensity decreases.

Test 5 Study Page • Summary

Solar System

Rotation

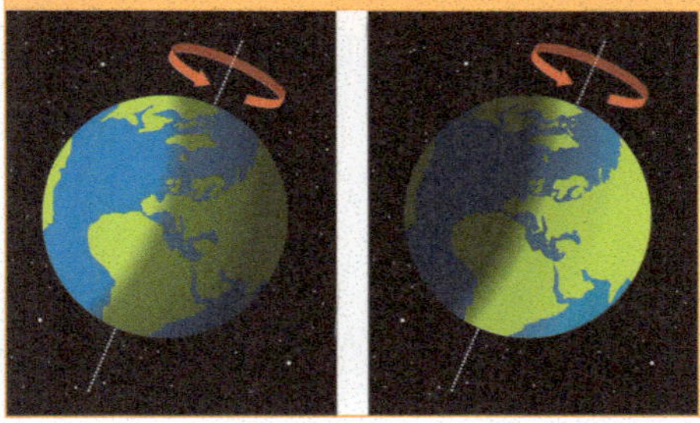

Earth spins on its axis approximately **every 24 hours** in a west to east direction. The main effect of Earth's rotation is **day** and **night**.

Orbital Revolution

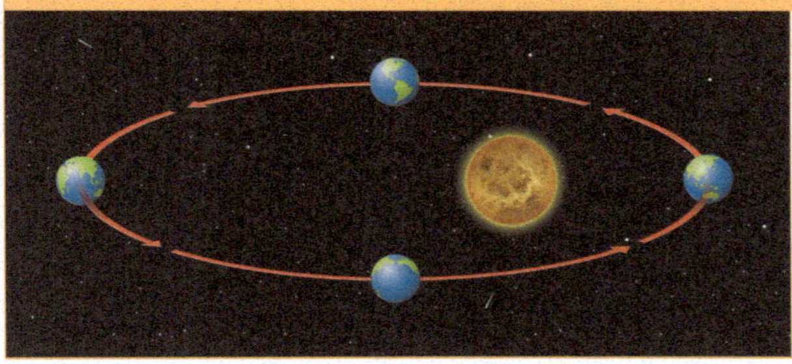

Earth revolves around the sun every 365 days, 5 hours and 49 minutes. The main effect of this orbital revolution is to create the seasons of the year. They are autumn/fall, winter, spring and summer.

Section 2

3. What are the effects of these movements of Earth? List them.

Rotation	_______________ _______________
Orbital Revolution	_______________ _______________

Section 3

4. Write **T** for true and **F** for false. If it is false, explain why.

a. ______ Solar eclipses occur when Earth is between the sun and the moon.

____

b. ______ The moon is not seen from Earth when it is in the new moon phase.

____

c. ______ The phases of the moon include new moon, waxing crescent, full moon, waning crescent.

____

d. ______ In a total solar eclipse, Earth completely covers the sun.

____

glue here

glue here

glue here

glue here

glue here

Test 5 Study Page • Review

Remove, complete, and glue in your notebook.

Section 1

1. Draw the planets in order of distance from the sun.

2. Antonia wants to represent and compare some of the planets in the solar system. To do this she found eight fruits of different sizes.

a. Which planet will the smallest fruit represent? Why?

b. Which planet will the largest fruit represent? Why?

Name: ______________________________ Grade: __________

Phases of the Moon

Waxing crescent	**Full**	**Waning crescent**	**New**

Solar Eclipse

This occurs when the moon is between Earth and the sun and projects its shadow on the planet. Solar eclipses can be annular, partial or total.

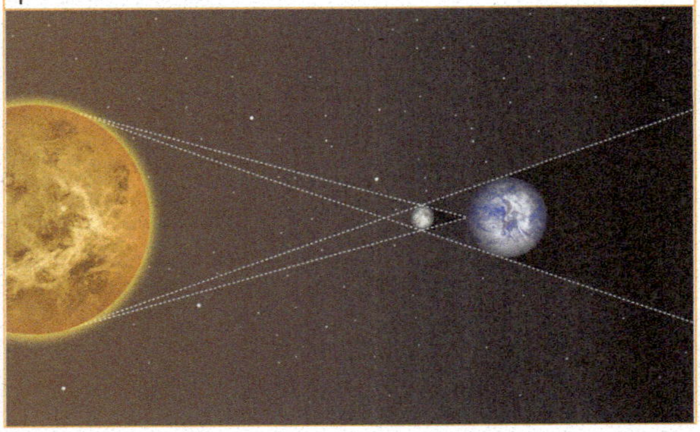

Lunar Eclipse

This occurs when Earth is between the sun and the moon and projects its shadow on the moon. Lunar eclipses can be partial or total.

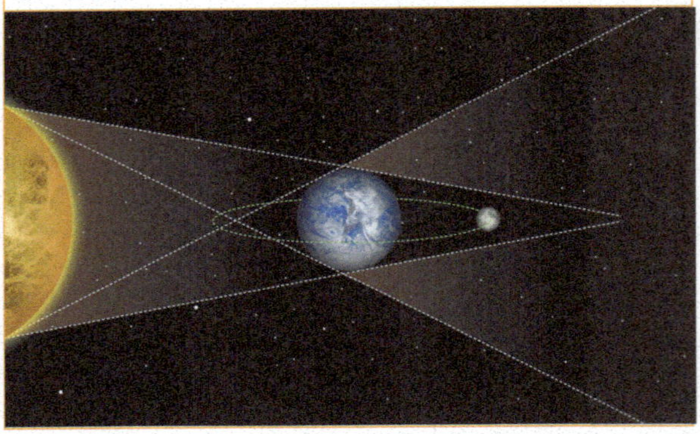

The Different Beaks of Birds

Activity Card 2

The Different Foods of Birds

Activity Card 3

The Skeletal System

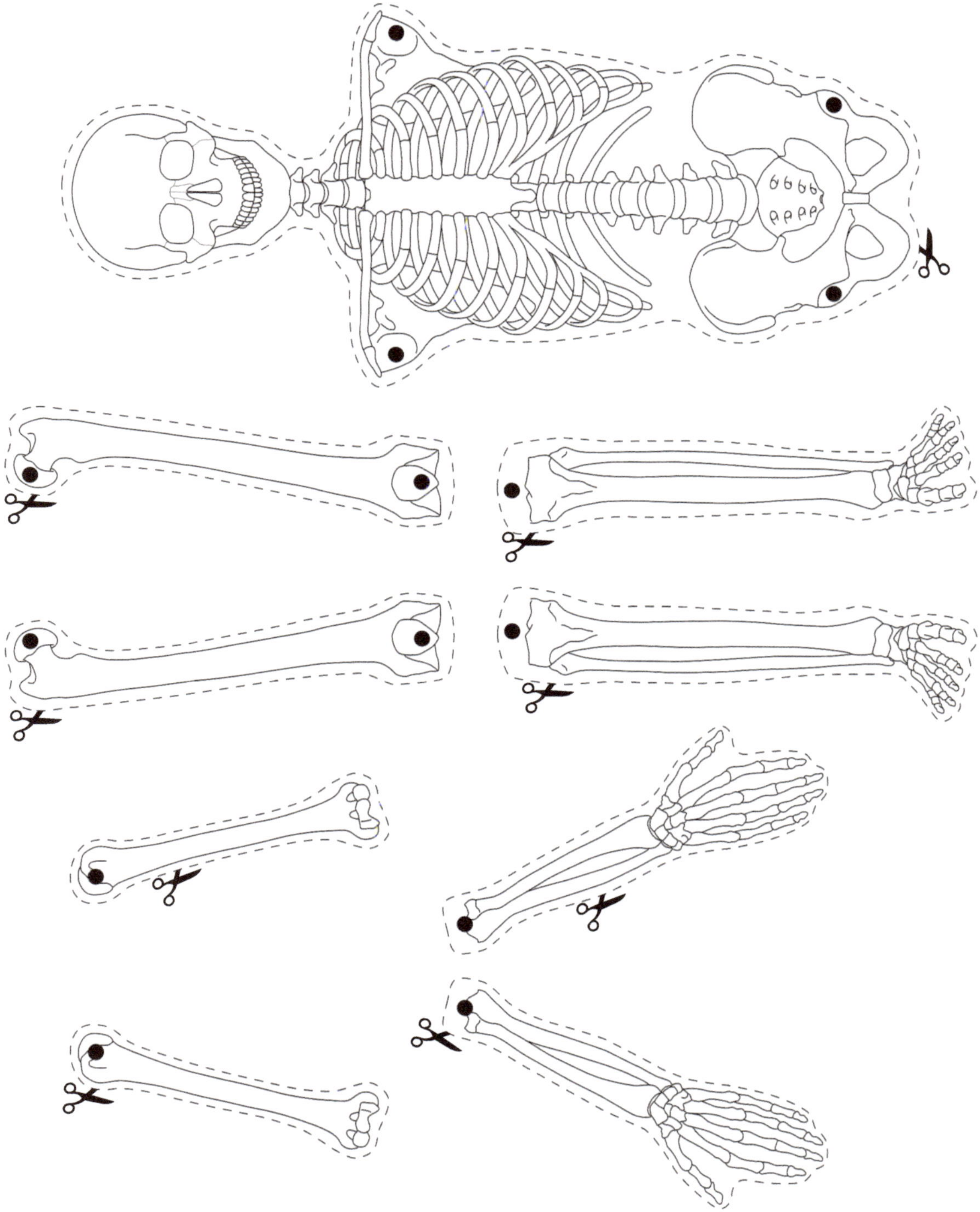

Activity Card 4

Model of an Arm

Supplies: scissors, 3 metal fasteners, red and blue string (30 cm of each).

Instructions:
- Cut out the pieces of Activity Card 4.
- Match the points 1, 2 and 3, and put a metal fastener through each.
- Tie the blue string to point C, and pull it through point A.
- Tie the red string to point D, and pull it through point B.

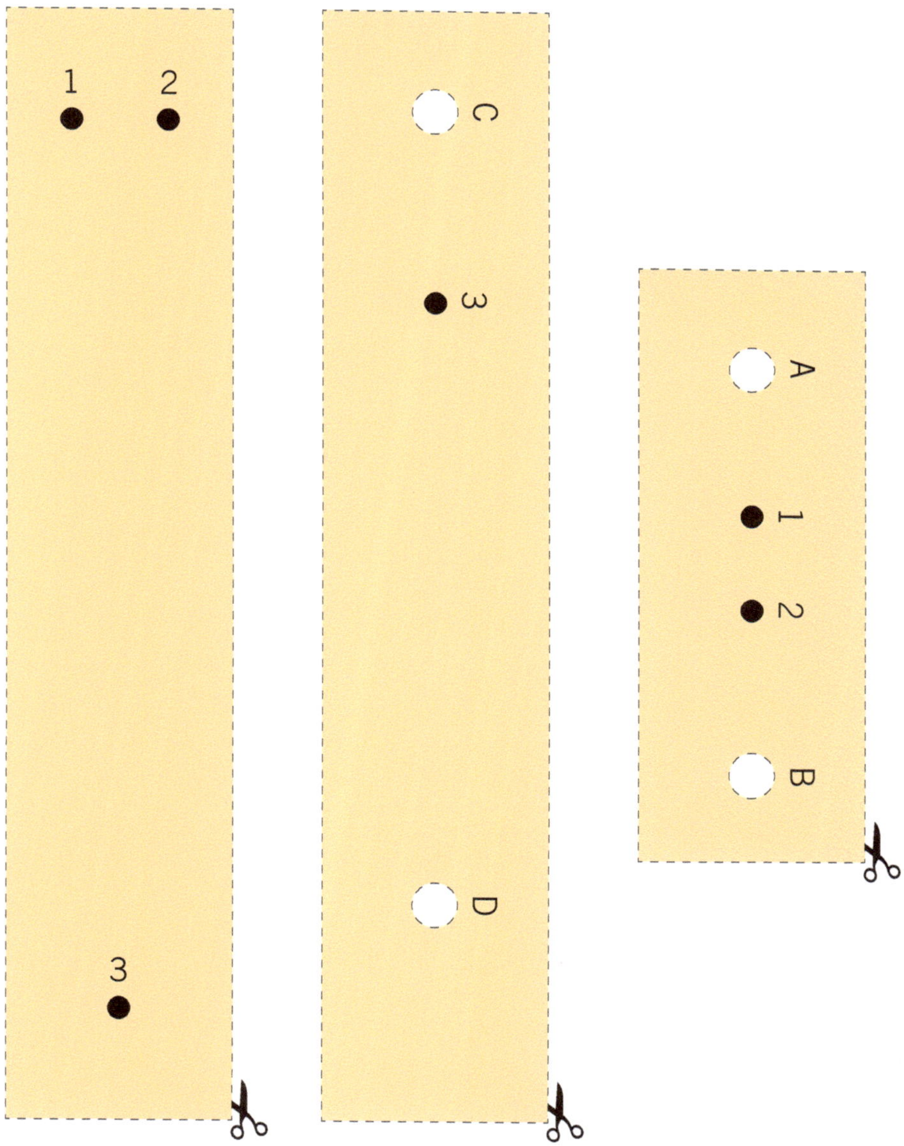

Memory Match Game (Nervous System)

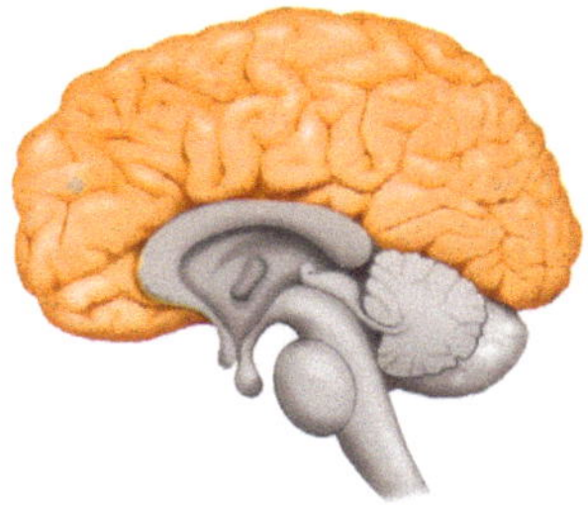

Controls respiration and circulation, also controls some eye movements.

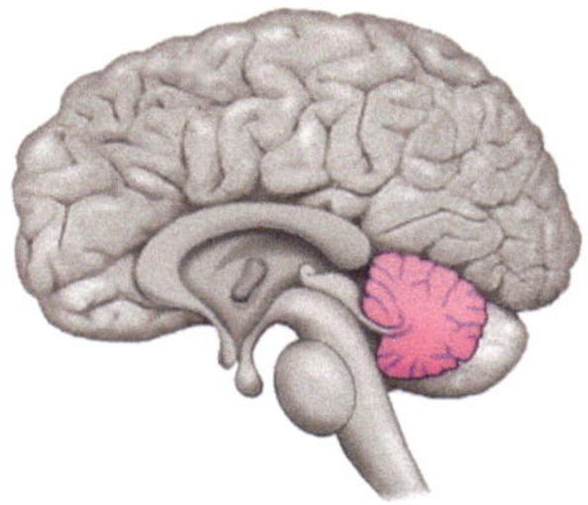

Controls functions like thinking and memory.

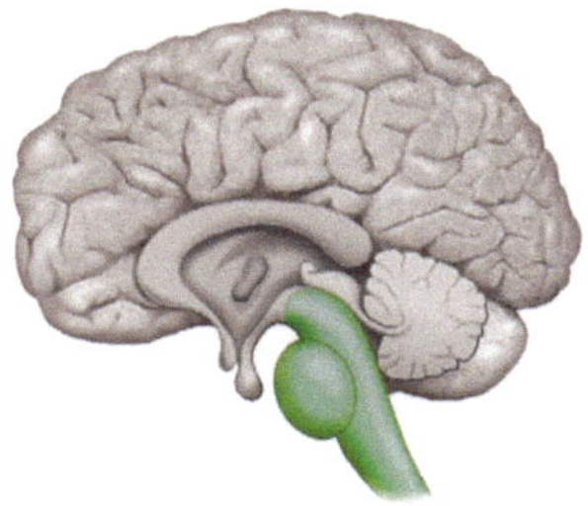

Conducts information to and from the organs of the nervous system located in the cranium.

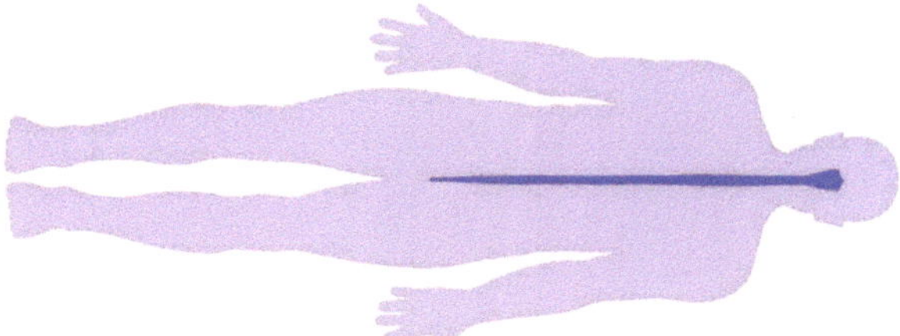

Coordinates muscular movements and controls balance.

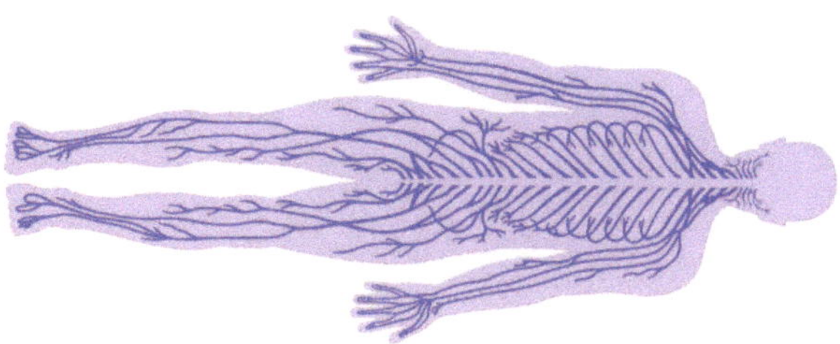

In charge of collecting and carrying information, located in all parts of the body.

Activity Card 6

Observational Report 1

1. Draw your observations.

test tube full of water	pouring water into the plastic cup	pouring water onto the plastic plate

2. What form did the water take?

____

3. Did the volume of the water change as it was passed from one container to the next?

____

Observational Report 2

1. Draw your observations.

test tube with an eraser in it	moving the eraser to the plastic cup	moving the eraser to the plastic plate

2. Did the eraser change its shape according to the container it was in?

____

3. Did the volume of the eraser change as it was passed from one container to the next?

____

4. What conclusions can you draw from this experiment?

____

____

Activity Card 8

Building a Spring Scale

Table of Equivalencies (hanging mass / applied force)

Mass (g)	50	100	150	200	250	300	350	400	450	500
Applied Force (N)	0.5	1	1.5	2	2.5	3	3.5	4	4.5	5

graph paper

Tectonic Plates Puzzle